2024 —

Josie!

♡ Mom

Endorsements

is a must read for anyone who desires to be about the Fathers' business. This book will lead to the culmination of a prayer like Jesus Prayed - "I have glorified you on earth by completing the work you gave me to do." My friend Greg will help you to get in Kingdom alignment for your Kingdom assignment. You will never be the same!"

RANDY CLARK

D.D., D.Min., Th.D., M.Div., B.S. Religious Studies
Overseer of the apostolic network of Global Awakening
President of Global Awakening Theological Seminary

Gregory Haswell's *Prepared for significance* is written as a parable, with an explanation in each chapter, to reveal how God prepares and trains people for His call on their lives. No matter which sphere of society God has called us to, He enrolls those He calls in a process of preparation. Understanding how this works brings relief, clarity and perseverance during this time of training. Those who do well are entrusted to be people who usher the Presence of God into their world. They get to pull the King's carriage. This book will help its readers gain understanding into God's dealings with them and encourage them to stay the course of His preparation. The powerful take-away principles found here are of great value. I found the book interesting, profitable, and easily understandable.

RACHEL FAULKNER BROWN

Director, Be Still Ministries

Rarely have I met anyone who has the kind of revelation about the kingdom as Greg Haswell does. *Prepared for significance* is no exception. To have this kind of vision around preparedness one must have lived out the pages of this book. Greg has been groomed, he has been trained by the audience of One and he knows team dynamics. This book is unlike anything I have ever read and is a modern-day kingdom leadership *Hinds Feet on High Places*. The honor of pulling the King's carriage is the honor of presenting Jesus to the world.

Dr. MICHAEL MAIDEN

Senior Pastor Church for the Nations, Phoenix Az

Author of "The Joshua Generation", "God of the Comeback", "Nothing but Jesus", "What is heaven saying?", "Turn the world upside down"

You're going to love this incredible book! In *Prepared for Significance*, Pastor Greg takes us on a wonderful parabolic journey about a team of horses which he uses to skillfully and systematically reveal to us great principles of the Kingdom of God. It becomes easy to see ourselves in this story, challenged and changed by the life-giving truths that pour out in chapter after chapter of this book. What a beautifully creative way to lead us on the road of discipleship. So many great biblical truths given to us in such a creative way! Read this book and meditate on the scriptural Kingdom keys and watch how your life will change!"

DALE L. MAST

you will find yourself more in awe of Jesus, more in love with Him, more confident of your place in His service, more at peace with the suffering you have experienced, and more eager to live as one who ushers in His presence.

JONATHAN JAY

Co - Founder of Maverick City Music

Many of the foundational values of Greg's personal life and ministry are given away in *Prepared for significance*. For anyone who is intending to live out the call of God on their lives through the work of ministry, this book is a must read. Greg's heart as an apostolic father, burdened with the responsibility to prepare the Lords bride until His return, shines through again. I can't recommend this book enough.

SUSAN HILLIS

Senior Leadership Team for World Without Orphans

Prepared for significance is an inviting, insightful, and inspiring parable that spurs us towards our own part in pulling the King's (Jesus') carriage to those destinies that fulfill our Lord's most glorious callings for our lives. The ongoing practical preparation through lessons of grooming, audience, and team are ones Greg and his family authentically model and live.

Through this book, we are invited in to share the unparalleled joy that comes through fully following the One who continues calling us forward.

ROD BROWN

Strategic Partnership Group-International

Greg's knowledge, wisdom, and creativity burst through the pages of *Prepared for significance*, as he shares how we become trained and equipped followers of Jesus. The parables Greg has created show us the generous way of our loving Father God and His desire to see us become all we were created to be.

ANDY COOK

CEO, Promise686

So many books hit your head before they hit your heart, or they fail to reach your heart altogether. Here you'll get both, and the encouragement you need to press into God's deeper purposes for your life. You are in this parable. *Prepared for significance* invites you to remember what's required to experience the depth of God's full plan for you through the pain and power that God alone can redeem and display. This is a story of Spirit-filled, time-tested Christian leadership. The type I aspire to display-- full of humility and most importantly, full of Him. Greg Haswell presents the story, backs it with Scripture and isolates practical advice for our growth.

The product is a refreshing step forward into God's deeper purpose for each of our lives.

STEVE BACKLUND

Bethel Leaders Network Associate Director

I highly recommend *Prepared for significance*. In this book, Greg Haswell uses his creative and inspiring teaching gift to equip us with the skills and mindsets to train well for the great callings and assignments of our lives.

Prepared for Significance

Enrolling in God's training process

GREGORY HASWELL

Deep Roots Press 2020

No part of this publication may be reproduced, stored in a retrieval system or transmitted in any form, or by any means: for example, electronic, photocopy, recording; without the prior written permission of the publisher. The only exception is brief quotations in printed reviews. Copyright © 2021 Gregory Haswell. All rights reserved.

Scripture taken from the THE HOLY BIBLE, NEW INTERNATIONAL VERSION®, NIV® Copyright © 1973, 1978, 1984, 2011 by Biblica, Inc.™ Used by permission. All rights reserved worldwide.

"Scripture quotations marked TPT are from The Passion Translation®. Copyright © 2017, 2018 by Passion & Fire Ministries, Inc. Used by permission. All rights reserved. ThePassionTranslation.com.

"Scripture quotations marked (NLT) are taken from the Holy Bible, New Living Translation, copyright ©1996, 2004, 2015 by Tyndale House Foundation. Used by permission of Tyndale House Publishers, Inc., Carol Stream, Illinois 60188. All rights reserved."

"Scripture quotations taken from the New American Standard Bible®,Copyright © 1960, 1962, 1963, 1968, 1971, 1972, 1973, 1975, 1977, 1995 by The Lockman Foundation. Used by permission."

"Scripture taken from the New King James Version. Copyright © 1982 by Thomas Nelson,Inc. Used by permission. All rights reserved."

Dedications

This book is dedicated to my wife Michelle, most gracious companion in the harness of God's call, the source of my most offered thanksgiving to Jesus, the one I most love to laugh with. Clothe yourself in splendor, gracious woman and ride out to victory.

To Nicole, my daughter of blessing, whose strength and wisdom bring constant joy to me, my pride and reward. Your clarity of thought, discernment, and ability to convey great thoughts with a few words continue to bless me.

To Tyler, my son in all but name, trustworthy and good, strong enough to say a clear "No!" to what he disagrees with, and too "weak" to put God's people into bondage, or to take advantage of them or to exalt himself.

Evangeline, most beautiful herald, whose coming marked the beginning of our seasons of joy and who continues to light up our lives. May God grant you the harvest of many years and of multiple generations.

Natalie, our new marker of the seasons of destiny, a weapon fashioned for her times and the living proof of God's faithful kindness and love.

Foreword

by Jack Taylor

The title of this book is the beginning of a graphic parable of far-reaching significance and is presented by one whose name is bound to become known because of this splendid work!

The setting is that of a traditional and carefully trained team of horses pulling a carriage with "Jethro," the principal steed in command. The whole picture then takes on the nature of what it means to be in service to the King.

The author lays down the picture of the Chariot of God's purposes and Kingdom with the indispensable results and responsibilities of those called to advance God's work. The introduction is not finished before it reveals an important connection with a vital conclusion: "Hey, He's talking about me... about us"! The rest will be clear.

Greg's processing of the parable is masterful and gripping. As you, the reader, gets it, you will never view ministry the same as before! When you lay this remarkable book down, you will be careful to notice Greg's name on any work from here on, and you will never pass the name "Jethro" without taking care to acknowledge your role in "pulling the King's carriage!" as you are "Prepared for Significance."

Thanks, Greg, for this clear and powerful reminder to us all of the meaning and might of our work in service to the King! We are waiting for more from you!

Jack Taylor

President, Dimensions Ministries,   Melbourne, Florida

Introduction

"There is a giant of a God in you, and He dreams great dreams for you!" I overheard someone saying this when I first met Jesus and it has been a helpful guiding principle for me.

God's dreams for us are fueled by His great love. His kind intentions for us are His operating system. He is always working everything out for the good of those who have been called according to His purpose. He means for us to be massively fruitful and His Spirit, living inside us, constantly leads us in the direction of His purpose. It is the dream of God for us that determines the dealings of God with us.

> **The dream of God for us, determines**
>
> **the dealings of God with us.**

His great dream for us so captivates His heart that He will not give it up. It shapes the way He works in our lives. It determined how He knitted us together in our mother's wombs, building in talents, gifts and personality traits that would be perfect for what He had in mind. That's why His gifting and His callings are irrevocable. He gave them as the raw materials to accomplish His desire for you. Seeing you brought into the full measure of that dream was part of the hope set before Jesus that allowed Him to scorn the shame of the cross. That dream for you remains the primary focus of Holy Spirit as He guides you in the way God intends for you.

It's this love-driven dream that fuels His dealings with us, even when we find ourselves disappointed by circumstances. Always ascribe to Him this glorious motive of love, especially when times are tough. When we don't understand, let's not make up theories and ascribe evil, anger, or malice to God's motives. Stay anchored in this understanding that in all things, it is His dream for us that He is working out in our lives.

When we understand that He's motivated by love, we must also understand that God disciplines the objects of His delight.

> **God's delight in us, is what**
>
> **motivates His discipline of us.**

This is clearly stated in the book of Proverbs which is repeated in the book of Hebrews in the New Testament.

> Hebrews 12:5 And have you completely forgotten this word of encouragement that addresses you as a father addresses his son? It says, "My son, do not make light of the Lord's discipline, and do not lose heart when he rebukes you, 6 because the Lord disciplines the one he loves, and he chastens everyone he accepts as his son." 7 Endure hardship as discipline; God is treating you as his children.

> Proverbs 3:11 My son, do not despise the Lord's discipline, and do not resent his rebuke, 12 because the Lord disciplines those he loves, as a father the son he delights in.

When we understand that the Lord disciplines His children like a father the son that he delights in, we avoid two extremes: becoming disheartened or despising His discipline. It is His delight in us that motivates His discipline of us.

Parents live with tensions. We want to protect our children from life's dangers and pain, and we also want them to be prepared to overcome the challenges life brings. We are proud when they stand on their own feet, pressing through tough times into success. The pain of watching our children struggle is eclipsed by the joy of watching them overcome. Our encouragements and words of affirmation are made real inside of them when they experience their own victories.

Our heavenly Father has these tensions in perfect balance. He is irrevocably committed to protecting us and at the same time, He calls for us to overcome. He wants to give us the gift of personal victory.

> **God wants to give us the**
>
> **gift of personal victory.**

This book stands in the tension of these two truths. Eagerly declaring God's faithful love, Jesus's accomplishment of a perfect salvation, and Holy Spirit's gracious instruction.

Even Jesus, God's only begotten Son, had to learn obedience through suffering. Though He was equal with God, He had to withdraw often to lonely places to pray. He was only released to minister after He was anointed with Holy Spirit but not before He had already lived without sin for thirty years. The spectacular and visible three and a half years of His ministry rested on the hidden thirty years of His preparation. You and I will follow our Master into that process of preparation.

God is committed to working in us what is necessary to sustain His work through us. He does this by teaching us something and then testing us to see if we've learned it.

> **God's is committed to working in us what is needed to sustain His work through us.**

Much like a teacher might do with a pop quiz, the Lord tests our hearts to measure progress. The tests are more for our perception than His, and they serve as markers of our progress and reminders of His love.

> 1 Thessalonians 2:4 On the contrary, we speak as those approved by God to be entrusted with the gospel. We are not trying to please people but God, who tests our hearts.

> **God's tests serve as markers of our progress and reminders of His love.**

Before we start, I would like to outline some basic presuppositions. If any of these is not settled in your heart, I suggest you wait before reading this book. The message and call of this book will be most effective when these foundations are in place.

Important basic presuppositions.

1. This sweat, pain, and effort is not about salvation

In this book I take as a given that you know who you are in Christ. The old you, marred by sin and sold into slavery, died with Jesus and the new, emancipated you has come. This new nature is made to be just like Jesus. You are filled with Holy Spirit, whose leadership demonstrates Jesus's nature through your personality.

Sin no longer has power over you because you are no longer seeking God's approval through the law but have forsaken that for grace and faith in Jesus's finished work on your behalf. God no longer views you on the merits of your own actions but by the merits of Jesus's actions, which He deemed to be perfect and which He declared to be completely acceptable. Now, because you are in Christ, you are wholly acceptable to God. You are blameless, holy, and free from any accusation. There is no basis for any boasting about your own efforts to secure God's forgiveness or approval. Now all you can boast about is the cross of Jesus Christ who has crucified you to the world and the world to you. Your salvation was secured, planned, executed, paid for, and administered to you by grace through faith. "This is not of yourselves so that no one can boast."

> **The effort and sacrifice explored in this book are not about working for salvation.**

I'm proceeding on the assumption that you know that your salvation is anchored on Jesus's work and not your own. The effort and sacrifice we'll explore in this book are not about working for your salvation. This book is talking about people who have accepted those truths and from that foundation, seek to usher in the Presence of our King.

2. We are all called to usher in God's presence in different spheres of influence.

There are many different places God could call you to serve. Although I am called to serve in the sphere of religion, this book is for people serving in any sphere of society (Media, Arts, Government, Family, Religion, Economy, Education, etc). Any call will adhere to these same basic lessons and tests. No matter where you serve, God is looking for prepared sons and daughters to usher His glory into the sphere of influence He has given them.

When I speak about those called, I assume you know that whichever sphere God called you to minister in is holy to you and to Him, and that there is no holier sphere than any others. Called believers in each sphere are tasked with invading earthly realms with Kingdom truth and wisdom. Let's not fall into the wrong perception that those following their call in the sphere of religion are more spiritual than those following their call to the economic sphere or the arts. What is spiritual is responding to God's call. The sphere is made holy by His call. It's your holiness in Christ that sanctifies the sphere. It is made holy by the habitation of the saints (holy ones) who respond to God's call to influence it. We need prepared Kingdom children to usher in God's glory in each sphere.

When our story talks about horses who remain in training and those who refuse it, I am not meaning people who serve in the sphere of religion are the called and those on the other spheres are the "paddock dwellers," a term in the book that is often used negatively. Unfortunately, many have wrongly taught this perspective. Thankfully, the church is learning to celebrate believers in every sphere. Paddock dwellers are those people called to each sphere who refuse the rigor of the training that will cause them to be effective for God's Kingdom.

3. Why the need for training and testing?

Let me put this in a modern-day parable. Imagine a successful entrepreneur, established in his privately owned multi-million-dollar business. His son, a vibrant teenage dynamo with great looks and personality, full of drive and natural leadership, shows interest in the family business.

Probably the worst course of action the father can take is to give that son immediate gratification of his every desire. Too much access to too many easy answers will probably be unhelpful to his development as an overcomer. The result will more likely be an undisciplined young man with unrealistic expectations, poor work ethic, and low character.

Not having to work for what he gets, exempt from knocks and pressures, means he will not likely display humility, compassion, clear perspective, perseverance, or any real understanding of the value of things. He will likely arrive at the family business expecting superior treatment for inferior results; after all isn't he the heir-apparent? What's more, this will probably not endear him to others in the organization.

Now imagine the same father who actively encourages his son to become someone worthy of respect. The son may have to work hard to fund some of his own college tuition. He must discover that a passing grade requires the discipline of study when his friends are out partying. He earns his degree by hard work, not an endowment to the college board from his father. He comes to work in the car that he bought and paid for himself. No special parking places await him, and he starts at the junior level and works his way up. This young man earns respect by his work ethic and character. His birthright does not excuse him from feeling the weight of his own mistakes. When he has been with the company for several years, he earns his seat at the boardroom table and after paying his dues, his father hands the company over to his control.

If you were an investor in this company, which son would you want to take the helm?

These two scenarios represent the difference between being a son and being a prepared son. The one relies on his heritage alone; the other celebrates his heritage but also carries the confidence of one who overcomes.

25

God is looking for over-comers, prepared sons and daughters, because He delights to hand His Kingdom over to them. He does not give His pearl to pigs, He does not reward casual inquirers, and He does not build His church on sinking sand. He develops mature children of the Kingdom and then confers on them authority. Many of them are battle-worn, often walking with a limp, but in their overcoming, they have discovered an aspect of the God who showed up when they called. They have wrestled with heaven, cried out in pain, believed through the darkness, and stood in the discomfort of integrity. Some may show less polish than we expect or exhibit scars from their struggles, yet they carry with them a distinct spiritual weight. These people usher in the presence of the King.

I know God to be wholly good, kind, gracious and abounding in love. I also know that He enrolls those who want to be used of Him into a training program that includes real struggles, pain, and pressure. These mechanisms train and prepare us to share the ministry of Jesus. It is enough for us as servants to be like our Master. But if we are to take up His calling and ministry, we will need to do it like He did, and we will suffer the same treatment from His enemies.

> Matthew 10:24 "The student is not above the teacher, nor a servant above his master. 25 It is enough for students to be like their teachers, and servants like their masters. If the head of the house has been called Beelzebul, how much more the members of his household!

To the mature sons and daughters, I pray this book will be life and encouragement. May this parable stir you to stay the course and cross the line in harness. I pray the words burn deep in your heart to remind you again that He is worth every minute of the preparation He invites you to.

It is one of the great passions of my life to encourage those who have given themselves over to serve our King. I see no greater hero, believe in no higher service, suggest no better way to give a life. Your destiny in God is so magnificent that it is going to require substantial preparation and training for you to accomplish it. It's going to require you to trust in the nature of the God who called you, even when circumstances make it feel like He has looked away from you. To you, the heroes of our faith, may this story be a bulwark to your faith, for this world is not worthy of you.

> Hebrews 11:35-38 Women received back their dead, raised to life again. Others were tortured and refused to be released, so that they might gain a better resurrection. Some faced jeers and flogging, while still others were chained and put in prison. They were stoned; they were sawed in two; they were put to death by the sword. They went about in sheepskins and goatskins, destitute, persecuted and mistreated-- the world was not worthy of them.

Chapter 1

The beginning of the road

PARABLE

The day broke full of promise. Jethro snorted and flicked his tail, stomping the early morning stiffness from his legs. Then, with a whooping cry, he charged off, waking all the horses nearby.

"It's here! It's here!" He sprinted around the field, kicking up his back legs. His mother smiled and called him back to nuzzle his neck. "Mom don't fuss, they'll see and think I'm a mama's foal."

"The King's men are not here yet," she said, "And even if they were, strong family relationships are something they admire."

"Do you think Uncle Malarok will be with them?" he asked, looking down the road where the King's men would arrive.

"Probably," she said, "He's one of the King's favorites, just like your father was."

Every time his father was mentioned, a grey cloud seemed to tug at Jethro's world, like a stain on the reputation of the chosen ones, the most honored among horses. His father had been one, a great prince and leader among them, but he had died in the traces, dropped dead while pulling the King's carriage. "He probably had a weak heart," thought Jethro with a little shame. Jethro shrugged off the heavy thoughts and whinnied at the scant clouds overhead.

For the tenth time, Jethro recited his own list of reasons why he should be chosen for the special training and acceptance to the royal school for horses.

"I am born of a royal line of thoroughbreds, an ancient unbroken line of special breeding. I am bigger than most, with a beautiful shiny coat, my mane is straighter and my tail longer than anyone my age in the paddock. I have strength, spirit and even the older horses make way for me when I run, and when I get up to speed, only Uncle Malarok can catch me. How can they not choose me?"

He looked around the paddock comparing himself with the rest and took heart. "They must choose me," he thought.

The sound of hooves on the road broke his line of thoughts and sent shivers down his flanks. The King's men appeared on the road, a long line of horsemen, riding the chosen ones, horses known for their breeding and training. They had all passed the training and been chosen to bear the carriage of the King. On each of their foreheads they bore a golden disk, the mark that they were chosen, a celebrated few from among the many invited to the trials.

All his life, Jethro had heard great stories of his father, Uncle Malarok, and others, but today, as he faced his own opportunity for selection, his earlier confidence began to corrode. They were impressive, disciplined, and bore such a calm authority that they seemed bigger than they were as they drew near.

All twenty of them turned at the same time and with an impressive display of perfect horsemanship, they pulled up in flawless unison and dismounted. Jethro saw Uncle Malarok and neighed his greeting, filled with nerves and excitement. Uncle Malarok, busy with this last maneuver, seemed not to notice.

"When I am one of the King's horses, I will have time to greet my own family and show them care and courtesy." Jethro thought with a sulk.

Now the selection process began. The King's men called each of the new horses to the center field ring and had them run around, watching their bearing and manner with great interest. Jethro couldn't wait for his turn to show them just how fast he was and how proudly he could tread.

"I'll show them just how this ought to be done. These old relics will have to make way for the new team, and we'll show them the way," he thought.

He stole a glance at the awe-inspiring line of King's horses patiently waiting at the edge of the field. As he gazed on, he thought to himself that they weren't all that impressive. "I think I can already do way better than most of them. After all I am faster, probably stronger too and some of them have hollows on their hindquarters, ugly marks where the traces and carriage pole has left its imprint."

It was rare that one of the King's horses did not bear these marks. It was how they were recognized when they were not wearing the golden disks of their choosing. Uncle Malarok had them, and in days past Jethro caught himself staring at this ugliness and wondered how they were acceptable to the King. Surely he would appreciate someone with a shiny coat and no marks far better than these marked old horses.

The crack of the whip snapped him back to matters at hand as the King's chief trainer called him forward. Jethro ran around, lifting his legs high, rolling his eyes and pretending that he was about to jump out of his skin.

"He has spirit and good lines!" the man said admiringly, "But will he pull in team?"

"His father was the great Jedediah, celebrated champion and his uncle is Malarok, the stout-hearted," came the reply from one of the older grooms. "He has the heritage and heart of kings."

"That remains to be seen," replied the calm voice of the trainer. "He will prove his valor or he will roam the wide paddocks." With the crack of the whip and a measured hand, the trainer made Jethro gallop and he sped around the ring, delighting to show his strength and speed.

"Woohoo! Look at him go," one of the young grooms cried. Their enthusiasm was not mirrored in the eyes of the chief trainer.

"Accept him and see to his grooming," said the chief trainer to one of the grooms with far less enthusiasm than Jethro thought he deserved. Yet elation filled Jethro as he was set aside with the other chosen horses. A gentle nudge from behind confirmed to him that Vincent, his best friend, had also been invited to the training.

"We are on the way, we are princes among horses, worthy of respect and acclaim," Jethro mused to himself. He stole a glance at his mother smiling her pride and hiding her fears.

At the edge of the field one of the King's horses mouthed under his breath, "If they knew what was in store for them, they'd be running for their lives."

This brought a chorus of snorts, gentle chuckles and a firm rebuke from Uncle Malarok. "Remember whose name you bear and do nothing to dishonor it," he said.

"You know what lies ahead for them," came their reply, "and all that swagger is going to get in their way. Most of them will not go the distance or demonstrate the heart. You know this, Malarok."

"I know it," said Malarok. "But don't take delight in their pressure and misfortune; we need many for the task ahead."

The selection process over, Jethro noticed that many horses had been invited to the training, and he cast an arrogant eye over the horses that trailed the King's men to the stables.

"There's not that much competition in this band," he muttered under his breath to Vincent.

"Yeah, but there is among them," said Vincent motioning to the orderly team of horses they followed. "They are very impressive."

The King's stables were like nothing Jethro had ever seen. Large ornate buildings, spotless and huge, overlooking the greenest pasture lands he had ever seen. Each of the new trainees was showed to a stall in the stable with fresh straw on the floors, blankets on the walls, and fresh water. Jethro loved it. The whole surrounding gave him a sense of importance he had not yet dared to believe was his right. But here, in this stable, looking out from his door, he knew he was born for this.

Looking through the gate, he saw a large paddock, filled with horses grazing the fields and playfully frolicking in the late afternoon sun.

"Who are those horses?" Jethro asked Uncle Malarok who was in the nearby stall. "Are they also chosen ones?"

"No," said Uncle Malarok "They are the paddock dwellers. They refused the traces for the open paddock."

Jethro looked up, unsure whether he heard regret or anger from his uncle. "You mean they chose not to pull the King's carriage? Can you do that?"

"For some, the training is too much. They want it to be about them, or they simply find out that they are not prepared to pay the price to be chosen. They refuse to obey, or they kick at the traces. If they fight

the role, or persist in rejecting the King's offer, they are led out of the training time to play in the fields."

"They seem happy enough," said Jethro.

"Oh yes, they are very well looked after, they do still bear the brand of the King after all," said Uncle Malarok. "But they never pull the King's carriage. They live in the satisfaction of their personal desires but also with the absence of real destiny. They lack nothing they need for a good life except the fulfillment of their greatest purpose. They watch as we bear the King's carriage, bringing His presence where it is most needed. Many of them are the most gifted horses alive and accomplish very productive feats. Most of them are very impressive in their own right, but they chose a lesser passion. They live near enough to His presence to boast and swagger to their friends, but not enough to convince them that they made the better choice."

Supper was served in a central area where four horses were gathered around feeding bowls of the finest foods. Two trainees were paired with two of the chosen ones. They talked with their mouths full, bright eyed and excited. Jethro and Vincent ate with Uncle Malarok and Jason, a large, muscular horse nicknamed "Fearless. "

"How did you get your nickname?" Jethro asked him over a mouthful of oats.

"I saved the King's life in battle," said Jason, "by taking a spear in the shoulder that was meant for the King."

Now Jethro noticed the scar that ran along his shoulder, an ugly mark marring an otherwise impressive appearance.

"You took it deliberately?" asked Jethro, who had forgotten to chew.

"Gladly! And I would do it again." For a brief moment, a fire lit up in the eyes of Jason the Fearless and a shiver rolled down the spines of the two trainees. A raw power, like a force of nature seemed to fill him, and they involuntarily backed up a pace.

"Your Uncle Malarok did a similar thing this past winter near the river and so have most of us here," he nodded at the chosen ones, the gold disk bouncing on his forehead.

"Of course, we have lost some who were not so lucky. Your father died pulling the King to safety with a supreme effort. He was my friend whom I admired, and a great horse."

For what seemed like the first time, Jethro noticed an assortment of scars, veiled limps, or indentations on the skin of the chosen ones. In fact, there was not one of them that did not show disfigurement or marks.

"You have all been in battle?" asked Jethro. A deep rumble of laughter began in Jason's belly, and he answered, *"Not one, many, hundreds even. We have seen more fighting and have been outnumbered in more battles that I can remember, without a regret."*

The fire was back in his eyes and Jethro shuddered thinking what it must be like to face that fire in battle. His bravado had melted into awe. He asked the question that had been on the edge of his mind since he arrived.

"Is it worth all this pain to pull the King's carriage?"

The two chosen ones looked knowingly at one another and then at Jethro and Vincent, *"And then some!"* said Uncle Malarok.

Just then, without a single command, without a sound being made, a grand change came on the assembly. The chosen ones stopped eating and straightened up. Some of the new trainees continued eating and talking, too full of their own thoughts to catch the change in *atmosphere. The King stood at the door, strong and well-dressed. Gradually and with helpful nudges from others, the younger horses quickly straightened up, amazed to see the King here. The King walked among them, looking at the new horses with eagerness.*

He stopped at Uncle Malarok and rested his head against Malarok's forehead while rubbing his chin. He whispered in his ear, too softly for anyone else to hear and pulled something out of his pocket and offered it to Malarok to eat. He turned and spoke to Jason, calling him fearless with a fond smile and patting his chest. He stooped to check Jason's forelock and nodded his approval at one of the groomsmen.

"It's healing well," he said.

The King then looked straight at Jethro with an approving eye.

"Now here is a foal I have had my eye on for a while," he smiled.

"He knows who I am," thought Jethro "The King knows my name."

"You stay the course and learn all you can from these around you," commanded the King, and then he added with a sad tone, "I would hate to lose you."

After the King's departure, they were all too excited to sleep. Jethro stood trembling in his stall, remembering those eyes on him and the sound of that voice. He felt as though his heart was filled up with courage and passion, like he could break through a wall or an enemy army or run forever. Yet what he could not let go of was the sight of the King touching his uncle's head and the whispered words between them.

"No matter what happens tomorrow," Jethro promised himself, "I will submit to the training to become a chosen one."

PARABLE DISCUSSED

Experiencing the call of God is intoxicating. It's a wild, heady ride of joy, anticipation, relief, hope, and passion. But the call is only the beginning. The call is the initiation into a life of training, a large-scale process of equipping those called in preparation for the responsibilities that await. God enrolls everyone He delights in, everyone He accepts as a child, into this journey. Take great encouragement from your training. It speaks a great word of God's favor and acceptance.

> **Hebrews 12:5-6 And you have forgotten that word of encouragement that addresses you as sons: "My son, do not make light of the Lord's discipline, and do not lose heart when he rebukes you, because the Lord disciplines those he loves, and he punishes everyone he accepts as a son."**

God's training program ought to be a cause of celebration, not discouragement. He is not a distant, distracted God who randomly dishes out misery because of our sins. No! He is astoundingly kind and loving but committed to working in us what is needed so that we can fulfill His purposes on earth. Within that process, He never leaves or forsakes us. He never walks away or rejects us.

God's call is intoxicating, and it's also His invitation to a life of training and pruning.

The gospel of God's grace proclaims that Jesus did for us what we were unable to do for ourselves. Jesus, the only creator of all things, the only eternal High Priest, the only begotten Son of God, accomplished far more than our feeble attempts at righteousness could. Embracing these truths does not exempt us from God's process of training. Rather, when we embrace these truths, they empower us to surge forward in the equipping of God so that we are ready to bear His glory in a fallen world.

Sowing to please God's Spirit is the only way to reap a good harvest.

We will eventually reap what we have sown. All of us live with the consequences of our decisions. Most of us have attempted the ineffective life strategy of sowing wild oats and then praying that the crop fails.

Yes, God's amazing grace does wash away a sinful past, but that same grace teaches us to live upright, self-controlled, and godly lives right here and now. So, while godly sorrow and repentance can wipe clean a foolish past, sowing to please God's Spirit is the only way to reap a harvest of good things in our future. We embrace our new nature, and with a renewed mind, pursue His dream for us. This is the theme of Paul's exhortation to the Galatians.

> Galatians 6:7 Do not be deceived: God cannot be mocked. A man reaps what he sows.

It is by grace we are saved, and God continues to view believers through the actions of Jesus, because believers are hidden in Christ. But it is obedience that allows us to become diligent stewards. Your actions and decisions matter in the outworking of your calling.

Your actions and decisions matter in the outworking of your calling.

Imagine two believers who are both recipients of Jesus's righteousness. If one is diligent in Biblical meditation and the other negligent, or one is a hard worker and the other chooses laziness, if one is consistently generous and the other embraces stinginess, they will end up in very different places in their faith walk. They may be equally qualified to inherit the Kingdom, but their responses to the circumstances of their lives will cause a different outworking of their faith.

All of God's people are born into a royal priesthood, to be part of a holy nation of God's children, called by the King to display His splendor. We have a remarkable pedigree. We have been born from above, marked in Jesus with a seal, destined to share a conqueror's throne, called to active service.

Many of us have a deep inner hunger to serve Him. Yet the difference between desire and action is measured by the price we are willing to pay.

Those who want to follow in Jesus's steps will be like their Master and will experience the same process He did. Those who want to usher in His Kingdom are called to pay the price to see it established in their world.

God is committed to preparing us and training us for all He has called us to. When we respond to His instruction, we become useful in His hands. Our faithfulness with what we currently have will determine the scope of what is still to come. Being effective in the service of the King has much more to do with our character than our natural abilities.

God is not that impressed with the gifts He freely gave us. He is impressed by our hearts and character, our strong and vibrant submission to Him. If all we really want to offer is our service on center stage, our gifts "sacrificed" in the full view of others, they fall way short of the glory He wants to bestow on us.

> **Effectiveness in God's service has more to do with character than gifting.**

It is often easy to see the scars on those who have gone before us—the marks of their labor in God—and wonder why God chooses to use them, even with all their weaknesses. Measured against our youthful enthusiasm, their accomplishments look small. This youthful passion, mixed with very little experience of hardship or failure, drives most of us in our early walk with God.

Yet after we have grown to a certain level, the day must come for each of us to be enrolled in the training to usher in the presence of the King. Jesus said that many would receive this invitation, but a few would be chosen.

A day comes when God no longer treats us like infants but offers to enroll us in training designed to make mature Kingdom people out of us. He wants people worthy of respect, honorable, trustworthy, disciplined, and responsive to His command. Youthful energy and naïve enthusiasm will not serve as motivators when the times are tough. The people required to usher in the Kingdom cannot be in it seeking to gain their lives. They have to be committed to losing them.

Some will enter the training and kick at the traces, spurning correction and fighting the lessons. If they keep this up for long enough, God releases them from the training to roam in wide paddocks filled with good things. I believe that because He is the kindest person we'll ever meet, He blesses those in the paddock with opportunities. They run around, kicking up their heels, free from training chains. Yet they will never bear the presence of the King into a crowd and will not be the people He entrusts to usher in His Kingdom. They have access but little authority.

> **Some will enter training and kick at the traces. They will have brief access but little authority.**

What does this mean? It means that God wants to use us for his purposes—to reach our neighbors, to pray for our coworkers, to share the gospel, to give to the poor, to encourage a friend—but He will use the people who are ready and willing. Like a good father, He will give His authority to the heirs who have learned humility and responsibility. Those are the people who will usher in His presence to a desperate world.

Once again, I emphasize this is not the harsh call of religion to service and pain, but an invitation to intimacy with Jesus, to share in His heart, being equipped for the mission He intends us to complete on the earth. Love is God's great motivator and the compelling force of our hearts.

The cost of the training will cause us to ask the question, "Is it worth all this pain, to pull the King's carriage?" The answer to that question will always be a personal one. Some will say it is, and others may think not. It depends on how close we draw to the King, the times of intimacy we share, and the secrets He whispers to those in harness.

We all get to make those decisions for ourselves, and we all walk in the consequences of the choices we make. The question at hand is whether we will submit to the training that is required to bear the presence of the King.

Tips to help us do well on this test

If many are called but few are chosen (Matthew 20:16, Matthew 22:14, Luke 6:13), and we are tasked with making our calling and election sure (2 Peter 1:10), here is a tip to make your election sure:

Cleanse yourself from things that would get in the way of where you're wanting to go. 2 Timothy 2:21 teaches that we have a responsibility to make ourselves useful to the Master. There are some things I choose to pursue and others I must choose to flee from. A great response to a calling of God is to engage in the direction of His call and filter out the things in your life that are detrimental to it.

Don't wait for someone to come and tell you to get rid of a particular worldly trait; cast it off and press toward the call. God's call is beautiful, but it will not do all the work for you. You must engage with it by showing yourself eager.

SECTION 1

The Lesson of Grooming

Romans 13:14 (NKJV) But put on the Lord Jesus Christ, and make no provision for the flesh, to fulfill its lusts.

Galatians 3:27 (NASB) For all of you who were baptized into Christ have clothed yourselves with Christ.

Becoming like Jesus is our highest goal. For us to bear His authority by praying in His name, we have to be clothed in Him. If we want to produce Kingdom fruit, we must embrace the identity we have in Him. Each one of us is His heir and His child. But each of us also has a unique identity in the Kingdom—the way He has created us and the way He sees us. This, we must also embrace.

The lesson of grooming involves two steps: throwing off what belonged to our old way of life and embracing our new creation selves. This is the lesson of grooming simply stated: we embrace our new selves and remove what displeases Him.

We have been put to death, buried, and resurrected with Jesus, and must learn to walk in the truth of this new way of life. We are brand new creations and we have been clothed with Jesus. Our bearing in this world should show it.

We are not called to show up dressed in our best attempts at righteousness and holiness and covered in condemnation. God did away with that faulty way of trying to present ourselves before God. We are called to be clothed in the Lord Jesus Christ, and His righteousness and holiness is now our clothing, beautifully sufficient to fulfill all the righteous requirements of God's law. This is not of ourselves, it is the gift of God.

If we still believe we live under the Old Testament's system of man's efforts to achieve right standing with God, we will never walk in the glory of the New Testament. Jesus said that the least in the Kingdom would be greater than John the baptizer, who was the best of the old covenant. Jesus said that our righteousness would have to be better than that of the Pharisees, who were impeccable at legalistic righteousness.

> **If we still believe we live under the Old Testament's system of man's efforts to achieve right standing with God, we will never walk in the glory of the New Testament.**

This radical renewing of our minds is vital if we want to usher in the glory of Jesus. The glory Jesus meant for New Testament believers cannot rest on Old Testament foundations. If we are to step into our new lives and the ever-increasing glory which is a part of our inheritance, we must know about the radical identity shift that happened when we were included in Christ.

Those who seek the authority of position but have not embraced this lesson of grooming cause damage. Holy Spirit is interested in grooming you as well as partnering with you for Kingdom causes.

Chapter 2

The Test of Appreciation and Disdain

PARABLE

The first day of training was not at all what Jethro had anticipated. He thought they would be learning battle tactics or how to prance and look regal. Instead, a groom arrived early before breakfast and began to groom the horses. First, the groom used a hard thistle brush to comb out Jethro's mane and tail. He washed him with a strange and intriguing soap, which came out of a box marked with the King's crest. After drying him off, the groom used a gentler brush to bring out the shine on Jethro's coat. Jethro had never had this much attention on his appearance. He enjoyed it.

Next, it was off to the forge for new shoes. He tried to look nonchalant as the new sounds and smells assaulted him, but he was nervous. The blacksmith was the largest man Jethro had ever seen. Jethro puffed out his sides in an effort to assert his authority. The blacksmith gave a muted laugh, unmoved by Jethro's antics. He leaned over Jethro's front leg and lifted it with ease to measure it for a shoe. Then, he went to the fire and banged on a red-hot iron shoe. Jethro, again, rolled his eyes and showed his teeth. But after the sizzle and smoke of a finished job, the blacksmith again came over and raised his leg for another measured fitting. At last, satisfied with all four shoes, he hammered them into place with steel nails and a big hammer. Jethro was released to a groom who led him out of the blacksmith shop, down the lane and back to his stable. The shoes were different but not painful in any way and Jethro liked the sound they made on the stone. Just as he passed Vincent, who was not yet shod, Jethro brought his feet down for added effect so that no one near could miss the fact that he was a shod horse of the King's stable.

Jethro was then surprised when a barber arrived at his stall to trim his mane and tail. They were once again brushed out to bring out their body and shine. A stable hand came in with a coat for him and slipped it over his shoulders, fastening it beneath his strong chest. Now Jethro felt like he was the most pampered horse in the world. Nothing like this ever occurred out in the paddock where he grew up. But now, here in these stables, he found himself avoiding mud puddles and the branches of the thorn trees because they would affect his appearance.

"I used to tease other horses that they were soft when they avoided the puddles and bushes," thought Jethro. "But it's different here in the King's stables. Everybody is watching me, and I don't want to spoil my new look."

Jethro was amazed by the changes in all of the trial horses. Each one was barely recognizable from the horses they were just a day earlier. Even their behavior was different.

The trainer arrived and charged the grooms to keep their horses looking good at all times. "They no longer represent themselves; they now represent the King and as such will be in your charge at all times," he said. The grooms seemed as eager as the horses to please. "Keep them well-groomed and healthy."

Uncle Malarok arrived and spoke to all the gathered horses in his deep voice, rich with authority. "Remember, horses, that you no longer represent yourselves. When you represent the King, only his opinion matters. You will conduct yourselves in such a way that brings him honor by both your decorations and your decorum. If not, you will be removed from this troupe and will be freed again to represent only yourself. Do you hear me?" he asked.

A chorus of agreement replied to him.

"This means that we steer clear from anything that could mar our appearance. We do nothing that will detract or distract people from the King's glory."

The chief trainer strode to the center of a training paddock with a strange looking set of chains. A line of grooms followed him, each carrying his own set of chains. "Set them in place!" The trainer ordered.

The grooms proceeded to attach the set of chains to each of the horse's legs and body. An unhappy chorus erupted from the nervous horses.

"Steady there!" commanded Uncle Malarok, "There is nothing to fear."

Once the chains were fitted, each horse discovered that as he moved his foot to take a step, the chains limited him. At the height of the step, the shortened chain made their ankles bend back toward them if they took their normal strides. This felt very uncomfortable at first, and some of the horses slipped in an ungainly display of clumsiness. Yet after a while, Jethro found a rhythm in it and discovered that if he cooperated with this new stride, it made him arch his back and prance a little straighter. He appeared to be gliding over the ground. He realized that the chosen ones all ran with this dignified gait.

Down the line, one of the new horses fought the chains, even biting at them in an effort to dislodge them. He reared up and tried to break free but fell with the effort and lay kicking and writhing, still chained. His groom made an effort to calm him, but he was unsuccessful. The chief trainer came forward in a display of courage, worked fast to dodge the flying hooves, and unclipped the chain's linchpin. The chains fell off, and the horse bolted. He ran around the training paddock, and then, as far from the chains as he could, stood quivering at the worried group who watched him.

"Give it another try tomorrow," said the chief. "If he will not accept them, take him out to join the paddock dwellers."

"Would they really send this horse away simply because he did not walk the way they wanted him to?" Jethro was astonished. "Surely the horse could be a help to the King without learning how to walk like they expected!" Jethro went to sleep that night worried at the prospect of his own dismissal and was determined to do well.

The next morning the chains were again fastened to their forelocks and they were made to run in them. Jethro found it easier than the day before. Yet the same horse who had balked at the chains the day before now struggled again. He tried to run but found that the restraint was unbearable, and he would not submit to them. Gradually, it became evident that he was not going to manage the chains, and the chief trainer gave the nod to have them removed. A solemn quiet descended on the gathering as he led the horse away toward the large outdoor paddock in the distance. On his way, the horse was belligerent and disdainful in his comments.

"This is all a huge waste of time. Get all dressed up like soft donkeys and made to prance like ponies that have lost their minds. I'm glad I don't have to be part of that insanity any longer. You can all keep your judgment to yourselves," he shouted defiantly as he was moving away.

Jethro felt no judgment toward him, only sympathy. The horses in training watched dejectedly as one of their fellow trainees walked out of their world.

But the training wasn't over. "Test their stamina!" cried the chief trainer. The horses were made to run around and around the paddock with their chains clinking and their coats shining with sweat.

"When do you think they will stop?" asked Vincent over his shoulder to a tired Jethro.

The trot that the chains enforced, though easier at first, became tiring and then plainly painful. A few of the horses began to show signs of giving up, tripping over themselves and slowing down. Just when Jethro was beginning to believe that he could no longer go on, the trainer yelled for a stop to the exercise. They had been running for a little over half an hour.

"Remove the chains and take them back to the stables," said the trainer. The horses were released and led back to the stables.

Uncle Malarok warned them to keep clean on the way home, "You are King's horses, keep yourselves from uncleanness and filth." But many were so tired that they passed directly through the puddles of mud in the middle of the road and uncaringly brushed their flanks against the thorn trees along the road.

"Surely they understand that we are tired and will excuse a little trudging," Jethro mused tiredly. It seemed that many shared his sentiment because most of them were looking decidedly scruffy and nothing like how they left that morning.

As they came close to the stables, some of the paddock dwellers were at the fence. "Look at the fancy clothes for the ordinary horses," they mocked. "They act all high and mighty, but they don't look like much to me."

"Yes," came the reply from another, "They thought they were far above us, acting all fancy for the last few days, as though being a new somebody means you can't mingle with us commoners."

Some of the trainees who didn't have enough self-belief to think they could make it through appeared sheepish before these taunts. Some of them laughed self-deprecatingly, as though their inner thoughts were in agreement with the jealous belittling of others.

Most of the trainees were so tired that they endured the mockery quietly as they cantered by.

Near the back came Uncle Malarok and some of the other King's horses. A sharp look from him silenced the paddock dwellers. Some of them tried to make up for their earlier remarks. "You truly are amazing horses; we've never seen any close to your magnificence." Somehow the praise felt even more malicious than the mockery.

"In both jeering and overt praise, they're still after their own agenda," Jethro realized.

When they reached the stables, they were not allowed to rest as a result of their condition and were sent back to their stalls for cleaning and grooming. "What a sorry bunch of horses," shouted the chief trainer when he saw their dirtied coats, "They're going to have to do a lot better than this!"

Dinner that evening was a far more somber affair. Many were sore, and most were anxious, daunted by the expectations and worried they were not up to the task. Uncle Malarok drew near to Jethro and a small group of horses standing together.

"Those horses today at the fence were a test for you," he said.

"They were just letting off steam I suppose," said one of the horses.

"No," said Malarok, "They were a far more dangerous foe than just a few careless remarks. Their words have the power to weasel down into the cracks of your minds and convince you that you are not who you have been chosen to be. These deceptive ways of thinking might just steal your whole future. They are thieves let into your minds, able to rip out what is starting to grow there. Do not play with them, resist them as much as possible! A truce with them means death to your destiny."

"So we can never speak to the paddock dwellers then?" asked one of the trainees.

"Of course you can," smiled Malarok, "We treat them with respect and gentleness, but we are careful with some of their perspectives which seek to steal our inheritance from us."

"We went for over half an hour today," Jethro told his uncle, trying to change the subject. "That's got to be some sort of a record, doesn't it?"

Uncle Malarok smiled, "For a first day, it's very good indeed."

"How long can you keep it up?" Jethro retorted, irritated by his uncle's indulgent smile.

"We once ran with the King's carriage throughout the great city for two and a half hours," said Uncle Malarok. "Now that was tiring."

In that moment, Jethro saw how small his triumph was and wondered at how the great horses even took time to talk with the trainees.

"None of you seemed to heed my warning to keep clean," said Uncle Malarok.

"We were so tired," snorted Jethro, "We were just trying to make it back home."

"It's what you do when you think the work is done that really counts," said Malarok. "If you are to be a King's horse, you will come to see that even when the traces are removed, even in repose, you still bear the golden disk of your choosing. It's not something you wear for a while and put off at inconvenient times, it's a mark of who you are, who you have chosen to become. The tasks may change but the calling remains"

Jethro felt dismayed. "I wonder if I'll ever be a great horse?" He thought.

After the meal, they walked back to their stalls where fresh hay and a clean blanket awaited them. They did not seem as luxurious as they had the night before.

"If this is all the reward we get for this much effort," thought Jethro, closing his eyes. "I'm not really sure if it's worth it."

PARABLE DISCUSSED

I guarantee that on your journey to becoming a living sacrifice, you will face the test of appreciation and disdain. These two are different faces of the same coin. They invite you to respect people's opinions more than the Lord's.

Many traps are set with a word of praise and appreciation.

> "Teacher, we know that You are true, and teach the way of God in truth; nor do You care about anyone, for You do not regard the person of men. Tell us, therefore, what do You think? Is it lawful to pay taxes to Caesar, or not?" (Matthew 22:15-17)

Appreciation and disdain are tests we must pass through. These tests teach us about our identity in Christ. They are goads designed to drive us away from an addiction to the opinions of people and into the arms of our

Father. His definition of us and how He sees us are more important than whatever opinions are popular culture. We need to practice the internal confession that, "I am who He says I am."

> **Appreciation and disdain are goading tests. They are designed to drive us away from an addiction to the opinions of other people into the arms of our Father.**

If we are going to serve Him well, we must be inoculated against the press of men's opinions and be motivated by His pleasure and call. This test measures our need for the adulation or praise from people against our desire to have the same from God. This is a key in being a true servant of our King. We need to actively seek God's approval and acclaim.

John 5:44 How can you believe if you accept praise from one another, yet make no effort to obtain the praise that comes from the only God?

> **There are going to be people on the sidelines of your life, who invite you to agree with them that you are less than Jesus says you are. Ignore them.**

There are going to be people on the sidelines of your life who will invite you to agree with them that you are worth less than Jesus says you are. Sometimes they'll do this gently, feigning concern, and other times with a sneer. They will make light of your calling, call into question God's choice of you, exert their opinion about your ability to accomplish anything. At times like that, we face a choice. We either come into agreement with their destructive purposes or we choose to agree with God.

The challenge in agreeing with God is that sometimes we might feel like the taunts of other voices are right. The enemy loves to remind us of our worst moments because he is a thief. He loves to tell us that we are powerless to change, and that the gospel is not transformative. Holy Spirit loves to remind us of our status as beloved children because He is the Helper. He reminds us that we are baptized and sealed in Christ, and that is our best moment and eternal state. He continually calls us deeper into glory and the unfurling of God's beautiful promise for our lives.

We must make a distinct choice to embrace what God has called us to and who He says we are. We must step into this truth by faith. It will cost us faith because all of God's work is done by faith. We are brand new creations in Christ, the old has gone and the new has come. We are beloved children, completely forgiven, blameless in His sight, and free from accusation. God means to bring great eternal fruit from our lives, for He chose and called us for this very reason. The amen must be spoken by us to the call of God on our lives. If we are hesitant or in agreement with the deceiver, we fall short of what's available for us.

To make the King's bidding our life calling, we must be willing to look both magnificent and unkempt if that's what service to the King requires, both glorious and disheveled in other people's eyes, because we choose to obey the Lord's command.

> **We must make a distinct choice to embrace what God has called us to and who He says we are. Calling and identity are linked.**

Many good people, called people, have excused themselves from the traces because they could not make peace with the fact that others may look down on them. They expected, in line with Scripture, that their service to the Lord would be held in high regard in love, only to discover that it was mixed with more contempt, mockery, and ridicule than they realized. They wanted the glory without the restrictions God's call had placed on them.

There are 17 things that 1 Tim 3:1-7 teaches must be true about those who desire to be overseers in the church. It is no use complaining that these are unreasonable or callous; they are God's requirements for those who sign up to serve. I have seen some people fight against these expectations, supposing that others will understand their particular set of circumstances. They justify their muddy spots and tattered places because they were tired or busy.

In my experience, the Lord will hold us to these standards when we are refreshed and when we are tired. Avoiding the puddles of mud at the end of the day is the job of great horses. Remembering the irrevocability of God's calling will help us stay true in public and in private.

Those who cannot respond to the constraints of service will never respond well to God's call to sacrifice. Those who will bear the presence of the King embrace all of God's call, even the sacrifice and sufferings Jesus said were part of our cup. This is the specific invitation of the servants of the King; this calling is a clearly stated theme of the New Testament.

> 1 Peter 2:20-21 But how is it to your credit if you receive a beating for doing wrong and endure it? But if you suffer for doing good and you endure it, this is commendable before God. To this you were called, because Christ suffered for you, leaving you an example that you should follow in his steps.

> 1 Peter 3:9 Do not repay evil with evil or insult with insult, but with blessing, because to this you were called so that you may inherit a blessing.

Yet these realities leave many tired and dejected and wondering if they have what it takes to survive. Are the few perks worth the pressures of the environment? Each of us must answer this for ourselves and more than once.

An illustration from our role in the church

Most people who have not been a salaried church worker do not know the hidden pressures of the position. Every time you appear in public, how you look, and act are carefully scrutinized and unlike previously, you are suddenly thrust into caring about these kinds of details that seem to be all important to others. A look, a misspoken word, or a joke at someone's expense can become a significant black mark against what most people presume should be a flawless character. We are led into a chain harness of do's and don'ts by a specialized customer base full of opinions on our form.

Many people just starting out in the ministry clean up outwardly, in their dress and their speech and their manners. Expectation bias is a strong taskmaster for those eager to do well in the King's business. But conformity to an outward behavior does not guarantee a strong and developed heart. In fact, unrealistic expectations, like a cancer, begin to eat away at our passion to serve the Lord and His people.

When we start in our calling, whether it be in the church, in business, or in any of the other spheres of influence, one of the first hurdles to overcome is the opinion of others. If we are not vigilant, their criticism or cynicism, which has no regard to what we have been through in service to the Kingdom, will slow us down or stop us completely. This kind of pettiness, constantly listened to, will wear down any sane person. I have seen many people who started to pursue the dream of God for them bow out purely because they refused to live under the constraints of other peoples opinions. While you are called to be a servant of God's people, they are not called to be your master.

> **You are called to be a servant to God's people, but they are not called to be your master.**

Your orders come from heaven. Your allegiance is primarily to heaven and your first love and obedience is to your King. The moment you are asked to do something that differs from the King's commands, you are free to ignore or refuse other people's expectations. It is amazing how often other people want to be the masters of your service. These people will have to learn that you love your King first and foremost and that you will do whatever He commands. While we love people and pour out our lives for them, we love Him more and are passionate about fulfilling His good pleasure.

> John 14:30 I will not speak with you much longer, for the prince of this world is coming. He has no hold on me, 31 but the world must learn that I love the Father and that I do exactly what my Father has commanded me.

Let people into the realities of your world. Tell them the stories of others who have placed unrealistic expectations on you. Have them join you in a project and do not shield them from the naïve comments of others. They will soon taste the lash of this whip.

> 2 Corinthians 8:21 For we are taking pains to do what is right, not only in the eyes of the Lord but also in the eyes of men.

We learn a more deliberate walk in front of others. A walking in harness. Sometimes it feels forced, along with a loss of personal freedom, but that is a small price to usher in the King's presence.

Tips to help us do well on this test

Decide to perform well whether people are watching you or not. Don't do it for their appreciation nor be discouraged by their disdain. Do the right thing when no one is watching because you trust in the God whose eyes look first to secret places to determine public promotions.

1 Peter 2: 18 Servants, be submissive to your masters with all fear, not only to the good and gentle, but also to the harsh.

Ephesians 6: 5 Slaves, obey your earthly masters with respect and fear, and with sincerity of heart, just as you would obey Christ. 6 Obey them not only to win their favor when their eye is on you, but as slaves of Christ, doing the will of God from your heart. 7 Serve wholeheartedly, as if you were serving the Lord, not people, 8 because you know that the Lord will reward each one for whatever good they do, whether they are slave or free.

Chapter 3

The Test of Identity

PARABLE

The next morning Jethro arose with fresh resolve. "I'll prove to the trainers and to the King that I am worth investing in," he told himself. Emboldened, Jethro stepped out eagerly into the sunlight of the new day. "Whatever they need me to do, I will do, whatever hardship I must overcome, I will succeed."

As the horses were taken out to the fields for training, they passed by the kitchen door of the palace. Jethro was surprised to see the King out so early talking to some men. He turned and called a halt to the procession of horses. Slowly, and with obvious joy, the King walked in among the trainees, stopping to rub a muzzle, look into a face or whisper into an ear. His presence seemed to fill the atmosphere with purpose.

Jethro became slightly jealous of horses closer to the King, with whom He spent time, or to whom He directed a smile or a whisper. Suddenly, the King was at Jethro's side. A hand settled on his bridle and the King's voice resounded in his ear.

"Hello there Jethro, the dauntless, what a great capacity you have. I'm going to need you to help out some of these others to make it through."

Great joy rushed through Jethro's heart; the King had spoken to him! He was so eager to prove himself, and yet with the horses all stationary and in this group, there was nothing about Jethro that could stand out. His speed, his strength, his appearance all locked down in this tightly standing group. Jethro could find no way to show the King his worth.

Soon the King moved on to other horses, smiling and encouraging them all. After a little while, the trainers had them marching on to the training area. The King shouted an encouragement to the whole group. "I am very proud of you!"

Jethro looked back, hoping to claim the praise for himself but was disappointed to realize the King had meant the group.

"How can He be proud of us? We haven't done anything yet. And how can He call me dauntless when He hasn't seen my strength?" Jethro asked himself. He wanted to earn the praise, and he was going to do his best to prove it was deserved. "I've got to discover the secret to why the King chooses particular horses. Then I will make myself acceptable and beloved in his eyes." Jethro thought long and hard. "He called me dauntless. I'm not so sure he got that right. How does he know who I am? Besides, there are some occasions I can think of when I was scared and the title dauntless surely didn't apply to me."

He remembered incidents where friends and older horses had teased him when he had got scared from a loud noise or with the appearance of a snake in a field. At both he had jumped, clearly spooked, and the derisive laughter from others at those times still had power to remind him who he really was.

"The King calls me dauntless but it's only because He doesn't know who I am, but I will change, I will earn His love." Jethro's thoughts brought him down, so he promised himself even more, stirring up his zeal, "I will be better than all these others."

At dinner that evening, Malarok bumped Jethro to shake him from his thoughts. "Hey there, young blood," he said, "What's got you so puzzled?"

"How can the King find such joy in that bunch of recruits?" asked Jethro. "Some of them are small and wimpy and probably won't last the week."

"You think the King's favor depends on perfect service?" asked Malarok, surprised. "The King loves because that is who He is. He is gentle and kind at heart, humble, loving, and faithful."

"But He was encouraging and kind to all and surely they don't all deserve it?" Jethro almost shouted.

"The King's response to those around him is not determined by their actions but by his choice to be who he is. He loves because He is a lover. He encourages because He is encouraging," said Uncle Malarok gently.

"But then how does he recognize talent and bring specific horses near? How does he choose?" Jethro's anguish was clear and his plea emotional. "I want to know how I can qualify for his love."

"You can't qualify yourself for his love Jethro," said Uncle Malarok with authority, "He has already qualified you to be loved. His delight in you is because he sees how you have been made, he sees who you are, and he delights in your design."

"He called me dauntless," said Jethro. "How can He say things that are unproven, when in fact the opposite has been proven on more than one occasion? How can He give love and acceptance before I could earn it?"

"Listen to me, young one," said Uncle Malarok quietly, "You are going to have to decide to either keep the identity you had before you

came to the King's stables or you're going to have to embrace the identity the King gives you. If you want to succeed here, my advice is to embrace who the King says you are. If you persist in defining yourself by past failures, you will not last here."

"So, I'm dauntless then?" retorted Jethro.

"Why yes, yes you are," said Uncle Malarok "I always knew there was something about you, and the King's definition has brought it into focus. I think it'll be your nickname from now on." With a smile and a chuckle, he ambled off.

But inside Jethro, something still yearned to earn a superior place.

PARABLE DISCUSSED

There is religious thinking that did not originate in God's heart, but it abounds on the earth. It sounds spiritual, misapplies Scriptures, and wins over many eager hearts. It *feels* right but is wholly wrong.

God does not accept us because we are perfect. His love for us, while we were still sinners, inspired Jesus's ultimate sacrifice on our behalf. It was because God **so loved us** that He gave His Son. God doesn't love us because Jesus died for us, Jesus died for us because God loved us. We don't qualify ourselves to God, **God qualifies us** to share in Jesus's inheritance.

> **God doesn't love us because Jesus died for us, Jesus died for us because God loved us.**

God's love for us is much deeper than our fickle performance. Peter the apostle declared with full conviction, that even though all the other disciples may abandon Jesus, he never would. Jesus told him that very same evening he would deny that he even knew Him three times. Fifty days past that incredible and public denial, that same Peter is leading the birth of the church. Reinstated by Jesus, he preaches on the day of Pentecost. For anyone reading this who may feel more like a paddock dweller than a chosen horse, take heart. Our God is the kindest and most merciful sovereign you'll ever meet, and He can reinstate those who come to Him wholeheartedly.

Those who are going to usher in the presence of the King need to be settled that it is not their love for God that holds their calling in place but His love for them. It is not their zeal, precious as it is, but His zeal that accomplishes eternal things.

> **It's not your love for God that holds your calling in place. It's His love for you that does that.**

Remember, we are dead to sin but alive to God. We are seated in heavenly places. We have a new nature and the old has completely gone. We have been blessed with every spiritual blessing in Christ. He sees us as holy and blameless in His sight, and our sins and lawless deeds He remembers no more. These will seem incongruent to the very real circumstances of our past. We will feel the bite of accusation from the slanderer shouting, "Don't you dare believe that! It isn't true about you."

We must learn the lesson of grooming by facing this test of identity. God will test our identity. Any identity not rooted in him will fall short of eternal purpose. He will call us and give us identity in Christ that we did not earn but must embrace.

> **Any identity not rooted in Him will fall short of His eternal purpose for you.**

Everyone who wants to bear the presence of the King must do so in the identity He has supplied. I cannot embrace the identity of myself as a depraved sinner because it is not who He says I am. I must embrace my true identity as a beloved saint. I cannot go on in condemnation, for there is none for those in Christ. Instead, I must revel in His acceptance and delight in me for I am now clothed with Jesus Himself, hidden in God, forever transformed into His image.

> **Everyone who wants to bear the presence of our King must do so in the identity He has supplied.**

I must embrace this new identity by faith and pursue it beyond accusations, slander, mockery, and doubt. The enemy wants to keep me in the identity I had when he had control of me. The Holy Spirit constantly reminds me of my new identity in Christ. I cast the deciding vote by agreeing with one of them. The wise choice is obvious. I choose to believe that I am who Jesus says I am and therefore can do what He says I can do.

Everyone God chooses comes to this test. Will we embrace what God has said about us and accept that identity? Many who face this test fail it a few times before they decide to believe what God says about them. When we believe, we identify with Jesus and clothe ourselves appropriately. Listen to how Paul accepts that his competence does not originate with his own efforts but with the working of God.

> 2 Corinthians 3:5 Not that we are competent in ourselves to claim anything for ourselves, but our competence comes from God. 6 He has made us competent as ministers of a new covenant—not of the letter but of the Spirit; for the letter kills, but the Spirit gives life.

Mary, the poor teenager from an obscure village, had to embrace her highly favored status with God. Jeremiah the prophet was told to no longer bring up the disqualification of his age or inexperience. Moses surrendered to his calling despite his rigorous objections. Joshua had to step into his role and do more than Moses could. Gideon had to shake off his fear and move out in the identity of a mighty warrior. David had to step into his calling to be King in order to destroy Goliath.

Until you embrace your identity in Jesus, you will not walk into the destiny He has for you.

Until you embrace your identity in Jesus, you will not walk into the destiny He has for you. Who God says you are is the enemy's primary attack. It should also be the most dedicated point of your meditation and confession of faith.

The Father told Jesus that He was beloved before He began His ministry. It was precisely this word that the devil constantly attacked. "If you are the son of God," the devil said, as if there was any doubt.

> **Who God says you are is the enemy's primary point of attack.**

This test of identity will come often. It comes to cement your identity in Jesus despite your circumstances, your own opinions or the opinions of others. We are who God says we are.

When David returned from killing Goliath, Saul kept his oath to give his daughter in marriage to him. But David refused because he could not see himself in that identity.

> 1 Samuel 18:17 Saul said to David, "Here is my older daughter Merab. I will give her to you in marriage; only serve me bravely and fight the battles of the Lord." For Saul said to himself, "I will not raise a hand against him. Let the Philistines do that!" 18 But David said to Saul, "Who am I, and what is my family or my clan in Israel, that I should become the king's son-in-law?" 19 So when the time came for Merab, Saul's daughter, to be given

> to David, she was given in marriage to Adriel of Meholah. . . . . 22 Then Saul ordered his attendants: "Speak to David privately and say, 'Look, the king likes you, and his attendants all love you; now become his son-in-law.'" 23 They repeated these words to David. But David said, "Do you think it is a small matter to become the king's son-in-law? I'm only a poor man and little known."

David did not step into his inheritance because he could not yet accept his new identity.

> **David could not step into his inheritance because he could not yet accept his new identity.**

But worldly religious thinking, what Paul calls the elemental spiritual forces of this world (Col 2:8), demands that we earn our identity. In this twisted thinking, we work hard to earn every accolade we get. It means that when I achieve, I have the right to boast and consider myself better than others. It makes us competitors with our brothers and sisters in Christ. This was why the Pharisees could look down on others, being harsh and judgmental of them while being proud of themselves. This is the most obvious decay of legalism.

The gospel of Jesus, however, settles God's love for us and our identity in Him on far more stable things than our efforts or desires. God's love and our identity are established by Jesus's perfect actions. I am loved and find identity from my faith in Jesus and not by trusting my own works.

Romans 11:5 So too, at the present time there is a remnant chosen by grace. 6 And if by grace, then it cannot be based on works; if it were, grace would no longer be grace.

> **The most obvious decay of legalism is the ability to simultaneously be proud of yourself – while being harsh and judgmental with others.**

This is what infuriates legalists. How could the Father throw a feast for prodigals and give nothing to the older brother? Because inheritance in the Kingdom does not come by works but by faith. Boasting is no longer an option for those who want to serve God because we do not qualify for God's love and acceptance by our own deeds.

Ephesians 2:88 For it is by grace you have been saved, through faith—and this is not from yourselves, it is the gift of God— 9 not by works, so that no one can boast.

I do not boast in my own works but in the work of Jesus on the cross. When I choose to let Him define me and I embrace His definition by faith, I give up any right to boast and I celebrate that with great joy.

Romans 3:27 Where, then, is boasting? It is excluded. Because of what law? The law that requires works? No, because of the law that requires faith. 28 For we maintain that a person is justified by faith apart from the works of the law.

> Galatians 6:13 Not even those who are circumcised keep the law, yet they want you to be circumcised that they may boast about your circumcision in the flesh. 14 May I never boast except in the cross of our Lord Jesus Christ, through which the world has been crucified to me, and I to the world. 15 Neither circumcision nor uncircumcision means anything; what counts is the new creation.

This was the great discovery Abraham made when the gospel was preached in advance to Him. He discovered that he was found to be righteous not by his own works but because he believed.

> Galatians 3:8 Scripture foresaw that God would justify the Gentiles by faith and announced the gospel in advance to Abraham: "All nations will be blessed through you."

> Romans 4:1 What then shall we say that Abraham, our forefather according to the flesh, discovered in this matter? 2 If, in fact, Abraham was justified by works, he had something to boast about—but not before God. 3 What does Scripture say? "Abraham believed God, and it was credited to him as righteousness."

Tips to help us do well on this test.

Gather two lists that will become the basis for your meditation, prayer, and confession. The first is a list of the life scriptures you have received, those scripture passages that seem to have great meaning to you and that appear periodically in your life. Capture these passages all in one place. Read, reread, and meditate on them and you will discover the Lord's direction for your life there.

The second list is a list of the things you know the Lord has spoken to you. If you are accustomed or in an environment where you can receive prophetic words, write out a list of these key words and promises that you believe the Lord has spoken to you. Just as with the life scriptures, read, meditate and pray about these. Speak out the promises and definitions you find in these two lists about your life. Take practical steps in the direction they point to. Exercise yourself in prayer along these lines.

Let me assure you, when you say about yourself what the Holy Spirit has been saying about you, it pleases Him and petrifies the enemy. When you claim what God has promised you, it isn't presumptuous, it is the beginnings of faith which always pleases God. Saying something other than what God says about you is presumptuous and displeasing.

On top of embracing our identity, we also give our best efforts to please Him. We make it our goal to please Him, but we never make the mistake of assuming that it was our own efforts that qualify us for His love.

Chapter 4

The dying test

PARABLE

Over the next few days, the training focused on stamina and fitness. It pushed the trainees to the limits of their endurance. They were often out after sunset, traipsing into their stalls and exhausted at the end of the day. On the fourth day of this rigorous schedule, they were taken on a long route that led them near Jethro's home. They passed the trial fields, and since they had come the long way, they were tired by the time the trainers called for an afternoon halt. Some inquisitive horses from the neighborhood strolled up to watch the trainees.

One of the surliest horses from the old neighborhood came up sneering. He had not been chosen as a trainee horse because he had hurt his hoof and could not attend the trials. Yet he was belligerent and mocking. His eyes scoured the group looking for horses he knew. When he found Jethro and Vincent, he mocked their appearance. "What a sorry looking group this is," he laughed. "And look at those two special cases. I'm surprised they could even keep up."

Jethro and Vincent both bared their teeth and flicked their tired heads. "Come over here and we'll show you who is sorry," said Vincent.

"We'll kick some sense into that thick skull!" said Jethro.

One of the trainers came over to them and told them harshly to settle down.

"He started it," thought Jethro with a flick of his mane. "We were just putting him in his place." The trainer looked at them sternly, and they settled back into their ranks.

But the mocking continued with renewed vigor. Several horses had appeared and were encouraging the mocker.

"Look at those spindly legs," he called loudly. "Don't you think they'll break the first time someone sits in their saddle? What an embarrassing sight! They thought they were big shots, they thought they were better than us. Well, they're no better than plough horses, a waste of the green food they eat."

Jethro lifted his head once again to reply, only to find a trainer slap his neck with the reigns. "Be still!" he commanded and would not leave Jethro's side. Jethro knew that he could outwit the taunters, he could intimidate them if he was allowed to go at them. "A short charge and a few choice derisions of my own would finish this," he thought.

But the trainer made it clear: being a trainee of the King meant that the freedoms he had once felt entitled to were no longer allowed for him. For the first time, he understood that the constraints of his grooming included his inability to respond harshly to those who were not part of the training. "This isn't fair," said Jethro. "We could finish this in a second if we were freed to do what we want."

"Yes, I'd love to put that puddle-jumper in his place with a swift kick," said Vincent.

"You two, stay behind with me for extra training," said the trainer.

"What did we do?" thought Jeht Jethro.

"I was named the most promising stallion of the vale," cried their persecutor as they walked away. "So much for you and your hotshot ways, Jethro."

Jethro knew not to respond and looked to the trainer for direction. The calm pat and smile of approval from the trainer gave him comfort.

"Yes, that's right, run along like a broken foal and do whatever your trainer says," came the mocking farewell. "And we thought he had potential, what a whipped loser!"

Jethro wished he looked better and that they had passed the field earlier in the day when he was well brushed and more rested.

On the way home, some horses crowded Jethro, bumping him once too often. He reared up and kicked out at the latest offender, scoring a solid blow to the chest of the horse who pressed him too closely. The horse went down because of the blow and Jethro felt a thrill of delicious pleasure that his kicks still had the power to make other horses wary.

The crash and sting of the trainer's whip shocked him back to reality. "There will be none of that among us," shouted the trainer. "Do that again and you're out."

Jethro was shocked. Didn't they see how he was provoked? Surely, they had witnessed his troubles. Why were they coming down so hard on him?

His trainer held Jethro back and led him into a large corral where he set training reigns to his braces and walked behind him to settle him. Jethro was too inside his own head to notice that another person stood quietly watching behind some trees. With a start, Jethro saw the

King watching. His head snapped up and he breathed deep and changed his gait.

"That's better," said the trainer and called for him to halt. The King came closer. "He got out of hand today," the trainer told him. "Not acting like a King's horse at all."

This angered Jethro because he knew it was true and yet it felt unfair.

"I hope he can learn these lessons," said the King." I know he can be one of the great horses." Then the King walked out of the corral.

Disgruntled, Jethro came back to his stall. Stubbornly, he kicked at the bucket in the stall and stomped in circles before he settled down. Uncle Malarok's head appeared above his gate.

"What do you want?" huffed Jethro.

"I'll come back when you are ready to behave," said Uncle Malarok.

Jethro felt like a fight. Horses and trainers had been provoking him all day. They had started what he was happy to finish and if he had just been left alone, he could have sorted all the nonsense out. He came to himself with a start. "Do I want to leave behind these restraints so I can go back to my old freedoms?" he asked himself. "No, I want to be a King's horse." He realized that he had to choose, and he did so right then. He trotted off to find Uncle Malarok.

"I've decided, I want to be a King's horse," he said after he had apologized for his surliness.

"Good," said Uncle Malarok. "Then I expect to see a new you and I don't want to ever see that old you again."

"What do you mean?" said Jethro.

"The old you that takes matters into your own hands, that bullies those weaker than you, who constantly positions himself in the best light and who never takes responsibility for his own actions."

"Was I really that bad?" asked Jethro.

"Now that you have decided to embrace the constraints of this opportunity, I don't think we'll ever see that horse again," said his uncle. "When you embrace the role of trainee, you have to let go of the old life you were free to live. Here, we don't spend every moment trying to assure ourselves that every other horse thinks we're wonderful. Here, we want to please the King. If, in that process, some others mock or tease or disdain what we do, we don't bite or kick them, we smile and bless them."

"So, they can but we can't?" asked Jethro.

"Exactly," said Uncle Malarok, "Where others may, we may not. They are not under our constraints, but neither do they get to hear about the King's business. Would you rather roam free among them, chasing down a high opinion of yourself, or be here with the King?"

"I'd rather be here," said Jethro.

"Well then, let go of the past and embrace the new. That horse you used to be before you accepted the calling is dead and gone and a brand-new future lies ahead here. Let that go so you can fully step into who you are becoming. "

PARABLE DISCUSSED

Our death comes to us by baptism, the baptism into Jesus's body done by the Holy Spirit when we believe. It is not by the efforts of our flesh. Flesh can only give birth to flesh and flesh can only kill flesh. If we want to crucify our old sin-soaked natures, it must be done by faith in Jesus's finished work. When we believed, it was accomplished by God's Holy Spirit as He submerged us into Christ and His death and resurrection.

> Romans 6:3 Or don't you know that all of us who were baptized into Christ Jesus were baptized into his death? 4 We were therefore buried with him through baptism into death in order that, just as Christ was raised from the dead through the glory of the Father, we too may live a new life.

If we want to embrace the training of God's Spirit, we will have to throw off what belongs to the old.

We died in a baptism, not through the effort of your flesh, so it comes to us by grace through faith.

Jesus's own hand cut away the depravity of the old and created in us a brand-new nature created to be just like Him.

> Colossians 2:11 In him you were also circumcised with a circumcision not performed by human hands. Your whole self-ruled by the flesh was put off when you were circumcised by Christ, 12 having been buried with him in baptism, in which you were also raised with him through your faith in the working of God, who raised him from the dead.

We now should actively live in the reality that we died and were raised with Jesus. We were baptized into His death and share it by faith. As we learn to become like Jesus, we will face this test of dying. We will be called on to prove that we understand we are dead to sin by dying to what once controlled us. We prove we died to our old nature, our old habits, and our old motivations when we throw them away and put them off. It is precisely our understanding of God's grace that enables us to say no to ungodliness. As we live in a world given over to sinful mindsets and temptations, we will have to remind ourselves that we have died to sin. This is the constant call of the New Testament.

> Colossians 3:4 When Christ, who is your life, appears, then you also will appear with him in glory. 5 Put to death, therefore, whatever belongs to your earthly nature: sexual immorality, impurity, lust, evil desires and greed, which is idolatry. 6 Because of these, the wrath of God is coming.

The cross of Jesus broke the power of sin and secured our new life, so we must come into alignment with that work by agreeing to cast aside the freedoms of the old and to embrace the constraints of the new. When we do, we discover the glorious, true freedom of the new, and we see, with clarity, the slavery of the old.

What a revolution this is. What the enemy warned was death is actually life and freedom in Christ. It is a glorious freedom we find in our new natures. So, we gladly throw off what belonged to the old.

> Hebrews 12:1 Therefore, since we are surrounded by such a great cloud of witnesses, let us throw off everything that hinders and the sin that so easily entangles. And let us run with perseverance the race marked out for us,

The Holy Spirit is a constant helper in this process. He helps us put to death the habits formed when we were slaves to sin.

> Romans 8:13 For if you live according to the flesh, you will die; but if by the Spirit you put to death the misdeeds of the body, you will live.

This is what Paul taught to the Ephesians. Put aside that old you, which is no longer appropriate and embrace the new. In this way, we become like Jesus. Anyone who wants to live in true, new creation freedom will face this test of dying.

> Ephesians 4:22 You were taught, with regard to your former way of life, to put off your old self, which is being corrupted by its deceitful desires; 23 to be made new in the attitude of your minds; 24 and to put on the new self, created to be like God in true righteousness and holiness.

Responses to temptation, destructive habits, self-promotions, or justifications of sin have become abnormal for those who want to carry the Kingdom into their sphere.

> Ephesians 4:25 Therefore each of you must put off falsehood and speak truthfully to your neighbor, for we are all members of one body.26 "In your anger do not sin": Do not let the sun go down while you are still angry, 27 and do not give the devil a foothold. 28 Anyone who has been stealing must steal no longer, but must work, doing something useful with their own hands, that they may have something to share with those in need. 29 Do not let any unwholesome talk come out of your mouths, but only what is helpful for building others up according to their needs, that it may benefit those who listen. 30 And do not grieve the Holy Spirit of God, with whom you were sealed for the day of redemption 31 Get rid of all bitterness, rage and anger, brawling and slander, along with every form of malice. 32 Be kind and compassionate to one another, forgiving each other, just as in Christ God forgave you.

I no longer have the freedom to deal as I want with those who press or mock me. Where others may, I may not. I no longer represent myself but am in training to usher in the presence of the King. I choose to put off malice, anger, brawling, bitterness and mockery, which were justified before I died. Now I embrace and celebrate my death to those things, because by that death, I have been emancipated from the old life of law.

The deeper we travel into the King's call, the more we must embrace this test of dying. It is a constant reminder to us of where we came from and the beauty that yet awaits us.

Jesus's great love, patience, kindness, righteousness and godliness are released to burst out into the world through our new nature. Mankind in Christ is back to original design. God did not merely cleanse us from our sins in Jesus and then say, "Go try harder." No, He cleansed us and then cut out sin, put to death our old nature and gave us new birth into a completely new nature just like Jesus.

> **God did not cleanse us from our sins and say, "Go try harder." He gave us new birth into a completely new nature created to be just like Jesus.**

Therefore, it is inappropriate for people who have become wholly emancipated from sin to walk in sin any longer.

Romans 6:1 What shall we say, then? Shall we go on sinning so that grace may increase? 2 By no means! We are those who have died to sin; how can we live in it any longer?

What have we learned? We cannot refuse the training and then expect the authority and power that comes with it. We cannot refuse to embrace our death and yet claim resurrection life. It's time to choose. We can't have both, and we can't keep old habits on the new man.

> **We cannot refuse the training and expect the authority and power that comes with it.**

It's time to agree with the crucifying work of Christ. Jesus told us to embrace believer's baptism and the Lord's supper. Both of these ordinances call us to remember our death, burial, and resurrection along with Jesus. In our baptism, we affirm our death, burial, and resurrection to a new life in Christ. In communion, we celebrate His death and ours in Him until He comes.

The embrace of this test of dying means we find glorious life in the new way.

> Romans 7:5 For when we were in the realm of the flesh, the sinful passions aroused by the law were at work in us, so that we bore fruit for death. 6 But now, by dying to what once bound us, we have been released from the law so that we serve in the new way of the Spirit, and not in the old way of the written code.

Tips to help us do well on this test

To break free from the crippling cycle of religion and the basic spiritual philosophy of this world, study the gospel of God's grace. Give yourself to the investigation of what Jesus accomplished on the cross and wean yourself from the idea that you can add a single bit of effort to improve what Jesus has already accomplished for you. Then, practice reminding yourself that your old self is dead. Jesus has given you His nature and made you brand new.

83

Chapter 5

The Test of Lordship

PARABLE

Jethro was a changed horse and it was apparent to everyone. He progressed well in the training and was celebrated by the trainers and other horses alike. The weekend came, a time for a break from all the training.

That Saturday, large and elaborate horse coaches started to arrive at the King's stables. Wealthy owners began milling around and the group of trainees were brought out to be inspected. The horses were picketed together in small groups.

Jethro saw out of the corner of his eye one of the trainers discussing him with an owner. The man strolled over to Jethro and tried to stroke his head. Startled, Jethro pulled back, looking for the trainer to show him what to do next.

"Woah there," said the man. "Come now, I won't hurt you."

Jethro wasn't sure, because although the words and tone were soft, he sensed something wasn't quite right.

"Calm down," said the man, "I can make your life wonderful."

Reaching out his open hand, he offered Jethro sugar cubes. Jethro had never had them before, but they smelled so good. He tried some.

A laugh escaped from the man as though he had accomplished something. That laugh made Jethro uneasy again and despite the fact that he loved the sugar cubes, he took a few steps back.

"I supposed this one is not useful at all," the man said and moved to offer his sugar cubes to another horse.

"What is this?" Jethro asked Uncle Malarok as he passed by.

"It's the day of the horse parade in town," said Uncle Malarok. "These are the wealthiest landowners in the Kingdom and they are interested in buying some of the trainees for their own stables."

"Can they just buy us?" asked Jethro fearfully.

"Not unless you want to go with them," said Uncle Malarok.

"Why would any horse want to go with them?"

"Their stables are elaborate, and their horses are treated extremely well. They are pampered and given the finest of foods."

"Do horses usually choose to leave the training for the parade?" asked Jethro.

"Yes, every year quite a few decide that they would prefer to be pampered than be a King's horse," answered Uncle Malarok.

Just then, another man approached Jethro. Jethro sensed the goodness in him and let himself relax a little more. The man stood in Jethro's eye line for a while, allowing him to get accustomed to him before he slowly drew near. Jethro could tell he had bonded with horses before. He began by gently speaking about Jethro's attributes.

"What a beauty you are," he said. "Look at those legs and your mane, you will be magnificent." He turned and called to one of his grooms.

"Wipe that mud off his forelock," he instructed, pointing to one of Jethro's front legs. "A horse this magnificent shouldn't be allowed to have mud on him."

Jethro was quite touched by this concern. Slowly and with measured movements, the man produced a cut-up apple. He offered it to Jethro.

Jethro leaned in and took the pieces from his open hand. His hand gently nuzzled Jethro beneath his face. Jethro liked the connection. The apple was the sweetest Jethro had ever tasted. The man offered more, which he greedily received.

"These apples are grown on my property, right behind my stables," he said. "They are the staple reward for the horses that please me. Would you like to come and be one of my horses Jethro?"

Jethro imagined the life being offered to him. It was far more than he had ever dreamed of accomplishing back at the farm. The man's horses were extremely well looked after. They were spoiled, watched over, pampered and prepped. Jethro thought of the envious looks those horses got from others, the preferential treatments at fairs and feeding troughs.

"That might be a great life," thought Jethro.

Just then, a commotion and a stir happened in the milling crowd. The prince of the nearby Kingdom came walking in their direction. He stopped with a flourish and rather arrogantly waved away the bows and acknowledgements of the people there.

"Let me see him!" he declared, looking at Jethro. "Yes, I think he might do. Certainly, the best I've seen today." He waved to a servant alongside him to make the necessary arrangements.

As the prince's groom came over and gently inspected Jethro, the first man who had given Jethro the apple bowed and walked away convinced that he could not compete with a prince.

"The first thing we would do is get you a blanket of better quality, only the finest will do." said the prince's groom. "Next, we'll get you cleaned up and brushed down. I don't know what kind of a stable they think they're running here but it is not the quality you will get used to. Clearly a specific diet will have to be developed. And you'll need a dedicated trainer."

Jethro noticed that the servant had the same arrogant air as his prince. Certainly, the list of improvements he could offer Jethro sounded enticing.

"But that's not all," he continued, and with a conspiratorial tone he whispered, "my prince is looking for his primary horse. His current horse is getting old and it simply won't do for the prince to be on an old horse. You could be the number one horse of the stable. The best stable, the best trainers, the finest food, and the most visibility."

It all sounded really great to Jethro. "The first horse of the stable," he thought to himself. "All the other horses deferring to me, having to fall in behind me." It was heady and exciting to think about it. This was the dream of any horse to be so cherished and pampered.

Jethro looked up to see Uncle Malarok looking at him from the far side of the meadow.

"If I go away from here, I will never be a King's horse, never get to pull the King's carriage. I will live a life of pleasure, but is that what I want?" Jethro thought.

With a start, Jethro remembered the promise he had made to himself and to his uncle. "I want to be a King's horse," he snorted. "I don't care if I'm not the first horse or eat sweet apples every day, I am perfectly happy with this blanket and these conditions, because I get to be with the King."

"Come with me," said the prince's servant. Jethro reared back and pulled his reigns from the man's hand. He startled himself with the ferocity of his emotion. But the attractive offers had come dangerously close to capturing his heart, and he wanted no part of them. Jethro cantered away from the man. Free from the picket line, he ran over to where Uncle Malarok stood.

"I don't like these men. I'm a King's horse," he said, loudly. Then, softer, "Sorry, am I making too much of a scene?"

Uncle Malarok had barely been containing his laughter. "You've done well," he laughed. "When I took this test, I actually kicked one of the groomsmen who tried to lead me away."

"This is a test?"

"Yes," said Uncle Malarok, "It's one that breaks my heart every time. Some horses are enticed away from the King's stable by fine sounding promises."

"Have any of your friends gone away to be horses in other stables?' asked Jethro.

Uncle Malarok showed real emotion as he answered, "A few did, but when we met again, they were barely able to acknowledge they knew me because they had become so pompous and arrogant. They were so caught up in their own self-importance that they often put themselves and their masters ahead of the King. They couldn't understand that their place was behind Him. They had become so accustomed to being served that the service of others, even the King, seemed foreign to them. Any gift or homage they make to the King is all about them and for their benefit and not for Him. They have become deluded by that choice. It has deceived and blinded them to reality."

"Why does this test exist if so much hangs in the balance?"
asked Jethro.

"If you want to be a King's horse, it is not only important that he
chooses you, but that you choose him, too."

PARABLE DISCUSSED

The test of lordship goes right to the heart of our identity. It examines the essential decision we all face concerning the tug on the human heart from both God and money. Are we going to be bondservants of Christ or merely pay lip service to Him while serving money? As we can only serve one of these two potential masters, we are all required to surrender one in favor of the other. If God is to be our delight, we will use our money to demonstrate His Lordship. If we secretly choose money as our master, it will demand that we surrender our walk with Jesus in deference to the lordship of money.

> Luke 16:10 "Whoever can be trusted with very little can also be trusted with much, and whoever is dishonest with very little will also be dishonest with much. 11 So if you have not been trustworthy in handling worldly wealth, who will trust you with true riches? And if you have not been trustworthy with someone else's property, who will give you property of your own? 13 "No one can serve two masters. Either you will hate the one and love the other, or you will be devoted to the one and despise the other. You cannot serve both God and money." 14 The Pharisees, who loved money, heard all this and were sneering at Jesus.

If we want to usher God's Kingdom into our generation, we must pass this test of lordship. The love of money is one of the most insidious strongholds the enemy can gain in a person's heart. It is the only thing that rivals God for mastery of the human spirit. The Pharisees sneered at Jesus, laughing and dismissing Him, because He did not share in their idolatry.

> Matthew 26:14 Then one of the Twelve—the one called Judas Iscariot—went to the chief priests 15 and asked, "What are you willing to give me if I deliver him over to you?" So they counted out for him thirty pieces of silver. 16 From then on Judas watched for an opportunity to hand him over.

Only those who pass this test are called to usher in our King's presence. Often those who fail become the Kingdom's worst opponents.

It was a love of money that drew Judas away from the miracles he witnessed. It enabled him to forsake the friends he had made, to be at internal war with his Lord, and to commit the ultimate betrayal. When people give their hearts first to money, they end up justifying their betrayals of Jesus. It often starts with jokes at His expense, putting Him, His people, or His Kingdom down. Watch for this in yourself and others. It's an early warning sign of a drifting heart.

The love of money is the only thing that rivals God for mastery of a human spirit.

> John 13: 27 As soon as Judas took the bread, Satan entered into him. So Jesus told him, "What you are about to do, do quickly." 28 But no one at the meal understood why Jesus said this to him. 29 Since Judas had charge of the money, some thought Jesus was telling him to buy what was needed for the festival, or to give something to the poor. 30 As soon as Judas had taken the bread, he went out. And it was night.

Scripture is loud about this point. Let's look at a few more examples. Demetrius the silversmith of Ephesus stirred up a riot against Paul and the gospel by using spiritual sounding arguments to disguise his hatred of them, because their preaching dug into his profits. He would rather perpetuate a profitable lie than embrace the eternal truth.

> Acts 19:24 A silversmith named Demetrius, who made silver shrines of Artemis, brought in a lot of business for the craftsmen there. 25 He called them together, along with the workers in related trades, and said: "You know, my friends, that we receive a good income from this business. 26 And you see and hear how this fellow Paul has convinced and led astray large numbers of people here in Ephesus and in practically the whole province of Asia. He says that gods made by human hands are no gods at all. 27 There is danger not only that our trade will lose its good name, but also that the temple of the great goddess Artemis will be discredited; and the goddess herself, who is worshiped throughout the province of Asia and the world, will be robbed of her divine majesty." 28 When they heard this, they were furious and began shouting: "Great is Artemis of the Ephesians!"

Similarly, a metalworker named Alexander stood against Paul and the gospel because it was in opposition to the money that came from idol sales.

> 2 Timothy 4:13 When you come, bring the cloak that I left with Carpus at Troas, and my scrolls, especially the parchments. 14 Alexander the metalworker did me a great deal of harm. The Lord will repay him for what he has done. 15 You too should be on your guard against him, because he strongly opposed our message.

Money has power. It creates a level of respect and influence for those who control it. This is part of the deceitfulness of wealth. It tempts us to trust in it, rather than to depend on God. It vies for space in our hearts and chokes out the words of Jesus. It colludes with arrogance. If we are not careful, it will corrode our heart for God.

> **Matthew 13:22 The seed falling among the thorns refers to someone who hears the word, but the worries of this life and the deceitfulness of wealth choke the word, making it unfruitful.**

Wealth is also deceitful because it pretends that it can provide everything we need. But money cannot purchase our souls, eternal fruit, security, or favor with God. Jesus said it is useless for anyone to gain the whole world but lose his soul. In Revelation, Jesus warned the church in Laodicea about the blinding effect of a love of money:

> **Revelation 3:17 You say, 'I am rich; I have acquired wealth and do not need a thing.' But you do not realize that you are wretched, pitiful, poor, blind and naked.**

Wealth challenges the Lordship of Jesus, so wealthy people especially need to be vigilant. Know this: God is not opposed to wealth. He is opposed to wealth's lordship over your heart. In order to follow God and build up worldly wealth in a godly way, we have to make a definitive decision that Jesus is our Lord. But be aware that this decision will be tested regularly by financial opportunities.

> **Mark 10:20 "Teacher," he declared, "all these I have kept since I was a boy." 21 Jesus looked at him and loved him. "One thing you lack," he said. "Go, sell everything you have and give to the poor, and you will have treasure in heaven. Then come, follow me." 22 At this the man's face fell. He went away sad, because he had great wealth. 23 Jesus looked around and said to his disciples, "How hard it is for the rich to enter the kingdom of God!" 24 The disciples were amazed at his words. But Jesus said again,**

"Children, how hard it is to enter the kingdom of God! 25 It is easier for a camel to go through the eye of a needle than for someone who is rich to enter the kingdom of God." 26 The disciples were even more amazed, and said to each other, "Who then can be saved?" 27 Jesus looked at them and said, "With man this is impossible, but not with God; all things are possible with God." 28 Then Peter spoke up, "We have left everything to follow you!" 29 "Truly I tell you," Jesus replied, "no one who has left home or brothers or sisters or mother or father or children or fields for me and the gospel 30 will fail to receive a hundred times as much in this present age: homes, brothers, sisters, mothers, children and fields—along with persecutions—and in the age to come eternal life.

> **Following Jesus with great wealth requires a constant surrender to His Lordship.**

The book of Numbers tells how Balak, the king of Moab, was terrified of the Israelites coming up out of Egypt under God's victorious arm, so he hired Balaam to curse the Israelites. Balaam was recognized as a prophet and someone who had favor with God. Obedient to the money, Balaam tried to curse Israel several times. Against the threat of losing the money, he suggested Moab set Israel up to bring a curse on themselves by enticing them to sexual immorality with Moabite women. Numbers confirms Balaam's responsibility for bringing about Israel's sin with the Moabite women, which resulted in idolatry.

Balaam came to represent the enticement of God's people towards both sexual immorality and idolatry in the New Testament. Balaam is mentioned three separate times in the New Testament. The first warns us of the **error of Balaam**. He turned to the way of financial advancement even though he knew it displeased God. His error was the choice of profit over God's pleasure.

Jude 1:11 they have rushed for profit into Balaam's error;

The second mentions **Balaam's way**. This is a strengthened position from a one-time error. A way is made by the continuous travel along the same path. Balaam made a habit of loving money and thereby placing God second to its demands.

2 Peter 2:15 They have left the straight way and wandered off to follow the way of Balaam son of Bezer, who loved the wages of wickedness. 16 But he was rebuked for his wrongdoing by a donkey—an animal without speech—who spoke with a human voice and restrained the prophet's madness.

The third mention is **Balaam's teaching**. This means that not only was it an entrenched habit, but he was now openly teaching it as though it were a respectable or viable option for God's people.

Rev 2:14 Nevertheless, I have a few things against you: There are some among you who hold to the teaching of Balaam, who taught Balak to entice the Israelites to sin so that they ate food sacrificed to idols and committed sexual immorality.

Balaam's error became his way. Then he developed teachings to justify it. Beware of Balaams.

Anyone who wants to usher the King's presence into the spheres of modern society will face this test of lordship often. Those who find their identity in the Lordship of Jesus Christ will be called on to demonstrate that lordship by how they handle their money.

Keep in mind that it's not the *amount* of money that is pertinent. Some believers will be called on by the Lord to the ministry of wealth. The question is not how much money we have but how much of us does our money own. We cannot usher in the presence of Jesus and love money at the same time. One will always be surrendered in favor of the other.

Those who usher God's presence into their generation have proven themselves in the test of lordship.

Godliness with contentment is a great gain.

1 Timothy 6:3 If anyone teaches otherwise and does not agree to the sound instruction of our Lord Jesus Christ and to godly teaching, they are conceited and understand nothing. They have an unhealthy interest in controversies and quarrels about words that result in envy, strife, malicious talk, evil suspicions and constant friction between people of corrupt mind, who have been robbed of the truth and who think that godliness is a means to financial gain. But godliness with contentment is great gain. For we brought nothing into the world, and we can take nothing out of it. 8 But if we have food and clothing, we will be content with that. 9 Those who want to get rich fall into temptation and a trap and into many foolish and harmful desires that plunge people into ruin and destruction. 10 For the love of money is a root of all kinds of evil. Some people, eager for money, have wandered from the faith and pierced themselves with many griefs.

Pulling the King's carriage, that is, bringing His presence into our generation, comes from those who have made Jesus their first delight. We do not let the promising shine of worldly wealth steal from us the real glory of heavenly treasure, or as Jesus called them, "true riches."

> **We cannot allow the promising shine of worldly wealth to steal the real glory of heavenly treasure.**

Hebrews 11:26 He (Moses) regarded disgrace for the sake of Christ as of greater value than the treasures of Egypt, because he was looking ahead to his reward.

Those who prove they have the correct value system are able to bring the treasure of heaven into the earth.

Matthew 6:19 Do not store up for yourselves treasures on earth, where moths and vermin destroy, and where thieves break in and steal. 20 But store up for yourselves treasures in heaven, where moths and vermin do not destroy, and where thieves do not break in and steal. 21 For where your treasure is, there your heart will be also.

The story of Esau provides an extreme demonstration of a calloused and dismissive heart toward heavenly treasure. For a single meal, he sold his inheritance rights as the firstborn son to his brother Jacob. Esau considered his inheritance worth very little. By the time he saw through his error, it was too late.

Hebrews 12:16 See that no one is sexually immoral, or is godless like Esau, who for a single meal sold his inheritance rights as the oldest son. 17 Afterward, as you know, when he wanted to inherit this blessing,

he was rejected. Even though he sought the blessing with tears, he could not change what he had done.

No matter which sphere of societal influence God has called you to, you will face the test of lordship. At some stage, you will be offered personal gain as an alternative to the call of God on your life.

Now let me say that for those who pass this test, the Father delights to bless them with everything they need to accomplish His dreams. Our Father is lavish in His generosity. He is the opposite of stingy. He is expansive and excessive in His expression of love. You can expect blessing from your Father in this area of money. In the process of receiving, always be guarding your heart.

Tips to help us do well on this test

As we cannot serve both God and money, one of them will be made subservient in our thinking.

We can easily take this test by examining which of the two we would discard at the threat of losing the other. If, at the possibility of losing my faith, do I find security in my money? Or at the possibility of losing all my money, can I find joyful security in my faith?

The one that is easiest to give up is a tell our hearts cannot hide.

SECTION 2

THE LESSON OF AUDIENCE

Learning to listen to Jesus

When we live our lives as though there is only one person in the audience, it frees us from the voices of other people and makes the voice of Jesus all important. Mankind truly lives by every word from the mouth of God.

If we want to bring God's Kingdom to our friends, our family, our neighbors and beyond, we must learn to value Jesus's words above all others, beyond our history and beyond our current perspective.

Chapter 6

The Test of Focus

PARABLE

Jethro and the others trained for two weeks with the chains until running with their forelocks arched and necks held high was second nature. It was time for the next lesson. All the grooms were gathered in a huddle and given instructions. The horses had been prepared earlier than usual and waited in the blankets on the side of the field. Uncle Malarok called them to attention.

"You are going to learn one of the most valuable lessons for a King's horse. It is the great secret to war and the foundation to your usefulness in pulling the King's carriage. If you miss this one, you are of little use and are potentially dangerous to the rest of us. Learn well!"

A fresh excitement thrilled though the ranks. The chief trainer gave strict instructions. The trainers fitted harnesses to each horse and then tied a tree trunk to each harness. These were heavy enough for the horses to feel their weight but not so heavy that they could not be moved. A course was presented to the horses, complete with obstacles, jumps, gradients, and waterholes.

"Each horse must complete this course by listening to his trainer," shouted the chief. Uncle Malarok was also in harness with a tree trunk and began to show the way. Jethro noticed that at key points in the course, large groups of stable boys and their families gathered. Uncle Malarok rode through the course. At some places he stopped, at some he charged, and at one place, he stood still for a full minute. His trainer had him lie down for a while at one hedge. At each point, the crowds cheered

and clapped and called out to Uncle Malarok. He finished the course to thunderous applause.

When it was Jethro's turn, he was eager to put on a good show. The crowd at the start called out his name and stuck their hands through the fence to scratch his coat. He was so busy responding to them that his trainer had to shout to get his attention. Once he started, his trainer told him to slow down. This irritated Jethro, who knew that his best attribute was his speed. He kept trying to speed up to show himself in his best light. His trainer was angry now, commanding Jethro to halt.

He halted and waited for the trainer's next signal. This halt brought cries of derision from the spectators. Shame welled up in Jethro who knew he could run through the entire course without being tired at the end. Why did his trainer not release him to do his best. Did he want him to fail?

Up ahead was a small jump. Jethro had cleared jumps three times that height and sneered at how gently the trainer had him approach it. Right then, the crowd above the jump cheered loudly and called for speed. Egging him on and chanting rhythmically. "Go! go! go!" Their enthusiasm sent tingles down Jethro's spine and despite the trainer's signal to walk, Jethro surged ahead and over the jump. He had just landed on the other side when the log he was dragging caught in the jump and he was yanked back to his knees. A loud chorus of jeers and scornful laughter washed over him from the crowd. The trainer helped him back up and an embarrassingly long pause followed while three groomsmen helped extricate the log from the jump. As the course progressed, another obstacle lay ahead. This time, there was a narrow pass on the one side and a large puddle of water on the other.

"I think we can make it through the narrow section," thought Jethro. "I'm sure that's what he wants." The crowd around the obstacle

stood pointing to the narrow pass and calling for speed. The trainer signaled Jethro to go through the water.

"It can't be," he thought and tugged against the reigns. The trainer was insistent and had to all but force Jethro's head on the right path.

"It will all end in disaster!" snorted Jethro and showed his displeasure with rolling eyes, a prancing gait, and tucked-back ears.

As he went through the water, he was surprised to see that it was only two inches deep and actually helped the trunk to slide, giving him a welcome rest. He also noticed that behind the narrowing path, there was a drop-off that would have been dangerous to him, especially with the log on his harness. The crowd booed him as he went by.

Next came the hedge where Uncle Malarok had been made to lie down. The crowd called for Jethro to lie down and made hand movements showing him how.

"They just want me to fail," thought Jethro. Then his trainer called for him to lie down, but he skitted about, wanting to know why before following the command. It was an affront to his dignity.

"There is no reason to lie down here, other than my trainer's power trip," thought Jethro. Eventually, when he became aware that he was causing a scene, he lay down. The crowd cheered him and applauded.

"I can't win with them," snorted Jethro. He finished the course in disgrace and turmoil.

"Failed!" cried the chief trainer touching the relevant horses with his whip to cement their shame. Jethro heard the word, felt the touch, and hating it for one moment, feared that this was the end of his training.

"Those who cannot learn to listen must leave by the end of the week," said the chief trainer. Jethro's relief and resolve swelled all at once. He had another chance.

During the following days, Jethro did better because he was determined to trust his trainer's voice and respond to it alone. Many times the crowd around him shouted their preferences, sometimes wanting to see him succeed and sometimes wanting to enjoy his public failure. He learned how to acknowledge them without giving them his attention. He knew that even a momentary lapse of attention could make him miss one of the trainer's commands.

Three horses were led out to the paddock at the end of that week because they would not listen to the commands of their trainers.

Late that night Jethro complained to his uncle.

"Why can't we think for ourselves?" he asked. "Is it always so important? Those were gifted horses."

Uncle Malarok spoke with a quiet urgency. "When you are carrying the King's carriage, crowds will surround you. They will want to pet you, offer you food and distract you. You must be trained for this. Loud noises, bright lights, the thrill of the crowd and the great cheer for the King, these are all distractions to the untrained horse. He will not hear the Master's voice. Those gifted horses were a danger to themselves, their team, and most of all to the King. More than once, the instant obedience to the Master's voice has saved the King's carriage from disaster. The bigger the occasion, the more obedient and focused the horses need to be. This is a basic of lesson of training."

"Once when riding with the King, assassins were sent into the forest to await us. The King had me lie down in a patch of brush for half an hour, hidden while they searched for us until reinforcements arrived

and arrested them. If I had been unwilling or slow to listen, we could both be dead. This is not a game Jethro. This is important," he continued. "Remember this the next time they applaud something you do. The crowd is fickle, but the Master is faithful. Remember this. Learn to receive your praise from the Master and eat from his hand."

"But aren't we supposed to represent the King well to the crowd?" asked Jethro.

"Yes, we must," said Uncle Malarok, "but while we are gracious to them, we keep our eyes on the Master and our ears dedicated to His voice. It matters not who else is cheering or sneering but whether the Master is smiling or not."

"I'll never respond to the crowds again!" declared Jethro.

"No! That's not it either," laughed Uncle Malarok, "The crowds love the King and we are called to serve them by bringing His presence to them. They are not the enemy, just not the best people to listen to for direction."

> **The crowd is fickle, but the Master is faithful. Learn to receive your praise from the master.**

After a brief silence, Jethro asked, "Uncle, with the risk of failure so high, is it worth all the training and hardship?"

"You'll have to figure that out for yourself, young one."

"Was it worth it for you?"

The deep rumbling chuckle was all the reply he heard, and it continued for as long as he could see Uncle Malarok walking back to his stall.

PARABLE DISCUSSED

The lesson of audience and this specific test of focus is one of the first we must learn if we are to lead God's people and usher in the presence of the King.

There are going to be many voices in the crowd, some meaning well and others harm. God will use people around us for love, wisdom, and encouragement, but what the Lord says must have a much greater weight in our hearts and minds. This becomes especially true the more successful we become, and the more people see us emerge in our sphere of influence.

> John 12:42 Yet at the same time many even among the leaders believed in him. But because of the Pharisees they would not confess their faith for fear they would be put out of the synagogue; 43 for they loved praise from men more than praise from God.

Those who will set Jesus apart as Lord of their hearts and listen to His word above all others will demonstrate wise spiritual choices.

> Romans 2:29 No, a man is a Jew if he is one inwardly; and circumcision is circumcision of the heart, by the Spirit, not by the written code. Such a man's praise is not from men, but from God.

Heavenly minded people do not lean on the praise or disapproval of the crowd. I believe God will lead all of us to this test of focus.

It's easy to see where people have set their focus by who they primarily give their ears to. Some listen to one voice from heaven, others will serve the many voices of the crowd. Heavenly listeners may discover themselves unpopular with the crowd, a state they are happy to embrace if it means the smile of their King. Without passing this test, we will not step into the full identity God has given us nor the call specific to our lives in His Kingdom. At no other time do we demonstrate more clearly whose voice we are focused on than when Jesus's voice is at odds with the voice of the crowd.

> **We most clearly demonstrate whose voice we are focused on when Jesus' voice is at odds with the voice of the crowd.**

There will be times when the audience loves what we do and times when they scream against us. When our gifting brings joy to them or meets their needs, they will cheer us on. But those who step into their role and calling know that the crowd who screams "Blessed is he who comes in the name of the Lord" at the beginning of the week can easily be screaming, "By what authority do you do this?" in the middle of the week, and "Crucify him!" at the end. Learning how to respond to people while listening for the King takes some practice.

Remember, we are in a Kingdom, not a democracy. There is one King of this Kingdom, One who will be exalted forever, One who is worthy. We do not share His authority as God, even though we are co-heirs with Him, nor will the crowd's democratic vote determine policy in His Kingdom. His will and His word are why this creation exists. All things were created by Him and for Him and all are sustained at His powerful word. Why would we consider any other voice on a par with His?

When we take to heart the crowd's praise, adulation, and honor, or their derision, criticism, and scorn, we find ourselves intoxicated with an inaccurate view. We are neither worthless nor useless, but chosen vessels appointed to the service of the King. At the same time, if we make poor choices, the Kingdom of God will not be destroyed by our inactivity or rebellion. The fickle nature of the crowd must not form the basis of our service.

Both praise and criticism form two sides of the same coin and are equally difficult to manage at a heart level. Harsh or mocking criticism of our purely motivated efforts is a bitter pill to swallow and most often does not reflect the King's heart.

We need to learn how to treat the two imposters of effusive praise and harsh criticism just the same. We hold them up for the Master's comment and accept His approval or correction. We become an easy target for the evil one if we take to heart the derision of bystanders. All the enemy needs to do when we are thriving in God is to motivate a swell of mocking or complaint to remove the wind from our sails. One glance over a shoulder to see the Lord's smile or to find His reassuring hand on our shoulder should be enough to push us through the tempestuous crowd.

Those who want to bring heaven to earth must learn to revere the Master's voice above all. We must honor Him as holy, revering His words as most pure, most powerful, and most trusted. This is the second danger of the praise of the crowd. It distracts us from the voice of the King. The excitement of the streets and the roar of approval can drown out His still small voice if we are inattentive.

Those who want to bring heaven to earth must learn to revere the Master's voice above all.

This is the constant warning of the prophet Isaiah.

Isaiah 8:11 The LORD spoke to me with his strong hand upon me, warning me not to follow the way of this people. He said: 12 "Do not call conspiracy everything that these people call conspiracy; do not fear what they fear, and do not dread it. 13 The LORD Almighty is the one you are to regard as holy, he is the one you are to fear, he is the one you are to dread,

Isaiah 50:4 The Sovereign LORD has given me an instructed tongue, to know the word that sustains the weary. He wakens me morning by morning, wakens my ear to listen like one being taught.

Isaiah 55:3 Give ear and come to me; hear me, that your soul may live.

God esteems those who have set His word above the applause of the crowd.

Isaiah 66:2 Has not my hand made all these things, and so they came into being?" declares the LORD. "This is the one I esteem: he who is humble and contrite in spirit, and trembles at my word.

There are many examples in Scripture of people whom God asked to do things that made little sense to them but who chose the word of the Lord above the applause or disdain of others. This is more fundamental to our service to the King than we have been led to believe. We must train ourselves to be people who tremble at His word.

Moses faltered at this hurdle and his leadership was removed from him. He did not listen to the Lord but responded to the people.

> **Numbers 20:12 But the LORD said to Moses and Aaron, "Because you did not trust in me enough to honor me as holy in the sight of the Israelites, you will not bring this community into the land I give them."**

This seems harsh to the casual observer, but it is the fundamental requirement for those who want to lead in God's Kingdom. Sometimes our own hearts will betray us to side with the crowd, not understanding why we are to camp again around bitter waters.

This is why we must be trained to respond to the Master's voice, knowing that He is faithful. The stresses and issues that challenge my heart now will in all likelihood be gone in five year's time, but Jesus will still be faithful and true. He sees what I do not see, He understands what I do not understand. His ways are always higher than mine.

So, we fix our eyes not on what we currently see, but on what we do not see, and we turn our ear to hear the still, small voice of our faithful Master.

The entire chapter of 1 Kings 13 is dedicated to explaining this lesson. It was this test that the heroes of faith passed with flying colors. Abraham regarded the word of the Lord as more holy than the circumstances of his life, believing God's testimony first.

Abraham regarded the word of the Lord as more holy than the circumstances of his life.

Hebrews 11:11 By faith Abraham, even though he was past age--and Sarah herself was barren--was enabled to become a father because he considered him faithful who had made the promise. 12 And so from this one man, and he as good as dead, came descendants as numerous as the stars in the sky and as countless as the sand on the seashore.

Romans 4:18 Against all hope, Abraham in hope believed and so became the father of many nations, just as it had been said to him, "So shall your offspring be." 19 Without weakening in his faith, he faced the fact that his body was as good as dead--since he was about a hundred years old--and that Sarah's womb was also dead. 20 Yet he did not waver through unbelief regarding the promise of God but was strengthened in his faith and gave glory to God, 21 being fully persuaded that God had power to do what he had promised. 22 This is why "it was credited to him as righteousness."

Paul put it this way in the New Testament.

Galatians 1:10 Am I now trying to win the approval of men, or of God? Or am I trying to please men? If I were still trying to please men, I would not be a servant of Christ.

> 1 Corinthians 4:3 I care very little if I am judged by you or by any human court; indeed, I do not even judge myself. 4 My conscience is clear, but that does not make me innocent. It is the Lord who judges me.

The harsh reality is that the current mood, desire, or action of the crowd is not our primary concern. Neither is our own mood or preference. Instead, what is primarily important to our destiny and well-being is His will and Word. The appeasement of the crowd and of our own concerns spring from the same root. They are a misunderstanding of the basic structure of things. The universe was not created for human beings; it was created for Jesus.

> Colossians 1:16 For by him all things were created: things in heaven and on earth, visible and invisible, whether thrones or powers or rulers or authorities; all things were created by him and for him.

The universe was not created for human beings: it was created for Jesus.

Without this understanding, we become servants who are quick to complain about the harshness of the expectations, yet we expect commendation and applause for the smallest obedience. This is not what Jesus has called us to.

> Luke 17:7 "Suppose one of you had a servant plowing or looking after the sheep. Would he say to the servant when he comes in from the field, 'Come along now and sit down to eat'? 8 Would he not rather say, 'Prepare my supper, get yourself ready and wait on me while I eat and drink; after that you may eat and drink'? 9 Would he thank the servant because he did what he was told to do? 10 So you also, when you have done everything

you were told to do, should say, 'We are unworthy servants; we have only done our duty.'"

The beauty and reward of setting God's voice above all others, including our own, is that we share the fellowship of the Master's business. He sups with us in the labor of the Kingdom, often stopping to share His heart with us. Here, our hearts find real joy and true peace. His counsel is devoid of selfishness, His rebuke life-giving, His whisper a roar in the heart. His smile and commendation is eternal, adding weight to what anchors our hearts in heaven. His ongoing fellowship leads us to places of satisfaction that the crowd has no access to. For it is true that eternal life is knowing God.

> **His whispers are a roar in the heart. His smile of commendation is eternal. He sups with us in the labor of heaven.**

God's servants must pass this test. As leaders of God's people, it is imperative that we keep our focus on Jesus and whatever He is currently speaking. If we don't, the pressures of leadership will prove dangerous to us and to those who follow us. This is part of the price tag of leadership. You will be asked to decide if it is worth it to you.

Tips to help us do well on this test

Build yourself a habit of valuing whatever Jesus says to you. Set value on His words by esteeming them above every other person's. If you are hearing the applause or the ridicule of the crowd, stop for a moment and sift through the voices. Which is a lie? Which am I responding to? What is Jesus calling me to do? Just as if two people are speaking to you at the same time and you ask the one to wait while you listen to the other, ensure that when others are speaking, you put them on hold and listen to Him.

Job 23:12 I have not departed from the commands of his lips; I have treasured the words of his mouth more than my daily bread.

Keep a journal of what the Lord is saying to you and make it a habit to do something each week as a response to what He has told you. This will develop a mindset that keeps His words of greatest value and sets the voices of other people in their proper context.

Chapter 7

The Test of Obscurity

PARABLE

A disconcerting shift began to take place. The trainers singled out some of the other horses for special attention. They were loudly praised, petted, and asked to go first. They barely paid attention to Jethro even when he excelled. It seemed that he could do little correctly. He was constantly given a comment or direction on how to improve. He took to doing extra exercises, being especially careful with his appearance, and even quieted his usual comments and digs about other horses.

"What has happened to you?" asked Vincent one morning. "You've lost your spark! I've never seen you this flat." Vincent was one of the horses now receiving more than his share of the training staff's attention. "I can give you some advice if you'd like," he said to Jethro. "It's simple, when you go near the trainers, you must hold your head up, skip a little to show that you're eager, and do what they say."

Jethro looked back at him. It was what he had tried for the last few days without any positive results. Nothing positive he did seemed to make any difference at all, but when he stepped out of line it seemed to be noticed immediately.

He went out again and tried his absolute best to accommodate the trainers, all while looking perky and obedient. Contrary to when he first arrived, these actions now seemed to produce scorn and not adulation. His attempts at eagerness appeared clumsy. The novice trainers blamed Jethro when he did not immediately obey their contradictory commands. They called him rebellious, stubborn. Jethro arrived back at his stable each evening more dejected and yet committed to trying harder. His frustration began to mount. He compared himself with the others.

"I'm far more intelligent than that horse, stronger than them all, and probably the fastest horse in the stables. I beat all their times on the obstacles challenge, and yet the chief trainer did not even comment."

Jethro had even been tempted to kick out at one of these horses when he had run too close behind him. He was running so close because he had taken it on himself to instruct Jethro on how to do better. It was clear to Jethro that in just about every area he could measure, he exceeded this bragging donkey.

That night, the King visited. What a commotion he caused. Uncle Malarok had been saddled earlier in the day and he and the King had ridden off to inspect reports of thievery a few miles down the road. They came back towards sunset and rode up to the stables. Uncle Malarok's loud guffaw was the first thing they heard. The King was leaning over his neck and speaking directly to him. They stopped, both laughing and in good spirits.

"It's time for a report on the new horses," the King said.

"Please don't ask the chief trainer," thought Jethro. Recently, it seemed the chief trainer had taken a particular disliking of Jethro. Always calling for more, always pointing out deficiencies, seldom was he happy. The chief trainer stood in the center of the stables and gave a commentary to the King on each of the horses as they turned to face each stable. Despite all their straining, the horses could not hear what he was relaying to the King. But his drop in tone was unmistakable as he looked at Jethro. What frustration Jethro felt.

"Nothing I do makes any difference," he fumed. "I don't seem to be able to affect any change on my circumstances." Jethro stood dejected and puzzled at the rear of his stall thinking about how much his strengths and gifts used to make all the difference.

Then, a voice nearby.

"Why are you not eager to see me?" asked the King, standing at his stall gate. Jethro came forward tentatively, not sure what to expect. The King reached out and rubbed Jethro's muzzle in a friendly way.

"Don't tell me that a little criticism is getting you down," he teased.

Jethro's heart leapt. The criticism of the trainer had not seemed to change the King's attitude toward him. He dared to lean toward the King, offering his neck and relishing the quiet moments they were sharing.

The King leaned in, rubbing his neck, and from the folds of his cloak, he offered a sugar cube. The trainers never offered these but for exceptional exploits.

"Now listen to me, my fine young friend," the King continued, "I see in you the heart of a great horse, but you still have so much to learn. Do not let your heart give out on you. Be strong, take courage. There will be many times you will have to wait for me. You must learn how to do this now. You are learning how to serve me well. You cannot serve both your needs and mine and carry on in my service. I expect you to endure right through all this training. Don't you give up on us!" And with that the King was gone.

Jethro's heart sang as he shook away the tears forming in his eyes. He did not want any comments from the other horses about how weak he was. His heart was alive, and his former broken spirit was renewed.

Yet the next day after the training, when some of the horse were called on to lend their strength to the chores around the stables, Jethro was given the most menial chore. His job was to clear the road of debris down near the muddy pool, at the place where the paddock and the road met. The surliest trainer came with him to supervise his efforts. Most of the trainees viewed the horses of the paddock with disdain. They had attempted the training and failed. Some of these horses jeered and teased as the King's horses and trainees went by. What little communication there was between the two groups was boastful and critical.

The paddock dwellers spoke of their freedoms and the wide-open spaces they had to run in. They were not restricted by narrow roads and hampered by the will of petty trainers. Some of them had done extremely well for themselves. They were sleek and unmarked by either the trainer's whip or the harness of the team. They trailed healthy and privileged families, born into the King's field of a royal bloodline. The trainees, on the other hand, boasted of their hardships in training, pointing out that they were still there; where many others had balked, they remained. The trump card for the trainees was their proximity to the King and the fellowship of sharing in His calling and suffering. Theirs was fundamentally a life given over to the service of the King whereas the paddock dwellers put other considerations first. It was usually here that the discussion broke, as there was no answer to this from the paddock dwellers. As Jethro and his trainer approached the puddle to clean off the road, a group of paddock dwellers gathered at the fence to watch.

"When you've finished that, plow-horse, you should also do something about that manure pile over there," said one tauntingly as he

nodded toward a pile at the end of the road. "It smells sometimes when we run on this edge of the paddock. See to it, will you?"

Jethro seethed and longed to retaliate but his training kicked in and he watched the trainer intently for orders.

"Come along boy, just ignore them," said the trainer with uncharacteristic gentleness.

They worked for half an hour clearing the way and making sure it was safe and comfortable for horses and people. It was about halfway through that Jethro realized that this road was most often used by the paddock dwellers. While he had been working, the paddock dwellers had been taunting him. The crowd grew in number and in confidence. They teased him, calling for more speed and pointing out any spot he had missed. They openly discussed his appearance and performance, causing him extreme embarrassment, shame, and anger.

"I will not fail here," Jethro told himself. "I will do well and go home with my head held high."

When he finished, a large horse from the paddock walked next to him on the other side of the fence.

"I wonder if this one can even run," he said. Jethro looked to his trainer with eagerness. He would love to teach this arrogant paddock dweller a thing or two about running. His trainer smiled and lifted the harness from him.

"Go on then," he said.

"Where shall we run to?" Jethro asked the paddock dweller.

"Do you see that large branch?" asked the large horse. It was attached to an oak tree that hung over the fence.

"About half a mile away?" said Jethro.

The horse nodded. "The first one to run underneath that branch is the winner."

"When do we start?" asked Jethro as his opponent snorted and charged. Jethro lunged and exulted in the joy of being able to run free and fast. Yet he was not far into the race when he discovered that the big horse matched his every effort. Even halfway through, the big horse did not seem to tire but exulted to run the course.

"I will not lose," thought Jethro, "For I am one of the King's horses. Imagine if I was beaten by a paddock dweller! They would probably exchange us and I'd be a paddock dweller and he'd be invited back to training."

Three quarters done, they came over a rise and at the last minute Jethro had to run around an obstacle that had not been visible from the start. The paddock dweller who had been ready for it, jumped the obstacle and took the lead. He was still three lengths ahead of Jethro when he ran under the overhanging branch. His taunting laugh hurt like hornet's stings.

"My name is Balarium, remember it well, trainee." He spat the last word as though it held very little respect in his mind. "You are not so haughty, now are you?"

"I have never been haughty!" said Jethro indignantly while catching his breath.

"That's not what my filly said the other day," said Balarium. "She said you tossed your head as you passed on the road when she called out for news of the King."

Jethro, feeling ashamed remembered his self-confident and superior attitude. "I'm sorry," he said simply. "Please tell her that it goes well with him."

Later that evening, Uncle Malarok visited Jethro as he leaned tiredly over his oats.

"I heard what happened today," he said. "Balarium was one of the finest runners around. Don't feel too bad that he beat you."

"He didn't beat me, he cheated," said Jethro defensively.

"Oh, I heard that he crossed under the branch ahead of you," said Uncle Malarok.

"Well yes he did but only because he knew the course better than I did."

"Whether through strength of limb or of mind, he still beat you," said Uncle Malarok with a gentle smile. Jethro merely nodded in defeat.

"How come I was sent to serve the paddock dwellers? They are inferior and worthless."

"You still see it that way after today?" Uncle Malarok shook his head. "They are neither inferior nor worthless. They have made choices for personal gain, but it does not diminish their worth or gifting. They are born of nobility, royal blood courses through their veins, their abilities and strengths are not diminished because they are in the paddock. They have chosen to spend their gifts enriching themselves and not in service to the King."

"Why must I, who has had the heart to endure the training this far, be expected to serve them?" persisted Jethro.

"We are not above them in value Jethro," said Uncle Malarok. "We are only more useful to the King because he can trust us. Besides, it's not them that you were serving but the King, who loves them and wants to bless them still. How his roads look reflects on him."

"I'm not sure I can handle being sidelined to menial tasks while others are cheered and celebrated," Jethro mused.

"It is in the little tasks assigned you, in the ones where there is no spotlight and no adoring crowd, that you prove your usefulness to the King," replied Malarok. *"Today, you did well."*

"So this is another test? The critiques and the ignoring?"

Uncle Malarok nodded, "What did the King say to you?"

"He told me not to give up on us," said Jethro.

"Then you have to decide if more time with him is worth the effort you are putting in."

"Will there be more like that?" asked Jethro.

"More than you can now understand."

PARABLE DISCUSSED

If we are the Lord's to command, we must learn to rejoice in His words and not merely the task He has commanded. We tend to want the most prestigious service posts, with profile, provisions, and praise at the ready. But if we exist for God's good pleasure, and He asks us to be His hands on the earth, then we will probably look a lot like Jesus, whose hands washed His disciples' dirty feet.

> **Jesus balanced the revelation that He was the Master of the universe with the recognition that He was called to serve.**

Jesus balanced the revelation that He was the Master of the universe and at the same time He knew He was supposed to serve. The test of obscurity teaches us this sober view of ourselves and reinforces our purpose.

There are other valuable results to the test of obscurity. The first is that it helps to ensure a sober view of ourselves. Away from the intoxicating cheers and self-serving flattery of the world, we sober up. Being sober is far less fun than having a drunk view of ourselves and is often the harbinger of harsh realities and disillusioning truths. But to taste this disillusionment implies that we were "illusioned" in the first place.

When sober, we see our own strengths accurately but also our own weaknesses. These bodies, with their feet of clay, house an all-surpassing glory in the presence of the indwelling King. We must learn that our own strengths and gifts are not the reason God chose us to serve and have relationship with Him. While valuable to the King, our strengths are not the reason He loves us. To think they are, is to believe that God's motive is to spitefully use us. No, the King invites us to be productive in ways that promote not only the Kingdom's good but also our deepest fulfillment.

When we see our own weaknesses, we marvel again at the depth of God's grace and love for us. We learn how to esteem Him and to view others and ourselves appropriately, neither as denigrated nor as demigods. These are the profound lessons of obscurity, which are seldom, if ever, found in the spotlight. Jesus takes us out into obscurity to show us our own hearts and to reveal His heart to us. This clarity is extremely rare and expensive.

> **Jesus takes us into obscurity to show us our own hearts and to reveal His heart to us.**

Most of us know in our spirits the sense and size of what God has called us to. This inner testimony can often intertwine with the whispers of selfish ambition. If we add to the mix a few well-meaning believers whose encouragement lapses into flattery, it starts feeding our flesh. Then, we start to imagine for ourselves a place where the true calling of God will not take us.

The test of obscurity brings with it this most profound blessing: the peeling away of a drunken perspective, replaced with sobriety.

Without sobriety, we are motivated by selfish ambition. We believe illusions created by overeager encouragers, people prophesying beyond their faith, or sometimes by our own imagination. We need to be disillusioned so that we can be "illusioned" by God's Holy Spirit. Obscurity will do this like nothing else. If you are in a season of obscurity, celebrate it and the amazing compliment it is from God.

This is His way with His people. When in obscurity, we find ourselves in the company of giants of the faith. Moses, who mighty in word and deed at age 40 (Acts 7:22), tried to accomplish what burned in his heart for his people. The result was death and loss of reputation and banishment into obscurity. Yet it was in this obscurity that he learned to be a very humble man (Num 12:3), even to the point that he did not think that he was any use to God. His obscurity ended with a call from a burning bush.

Joseph boldly proclaimed the call of God over his life, reveling in the dream of his father and brothers bowing down to him. Within a short space of time, he found himself in the bottom of a pit looking up at them. His time of obscurity lasted many years, but he learned a great dependence on God. He did not claim to be able to interpret dreams of his own power but assured Pharaoh that God could. His obscurity ended by a promotion to rulership and the fulfillment of his God-given dream.

Elijah was assigned obscurity for a while after his great pronouncement that no rain was going to fall except at his word. What a letdown from those lofty heights of command to be fed by the ravens each evening. The loneliness of that obscure brook is finally replaced with the ignominy of taking a widow and son's last bread. His obscurity ended with a consuming bolt of fire in front of the whole nation.

This is a test for us all. Yet in obscurity, the Lord does not leave us alone. He indwells and visits and encourages. The miracles of obscurity tend to be in daily provision, as Joseph discovered in the dungeons and David in the desert, Daniel in captivity, and Elijah by the brook. Obscurity is not the season of great visible demonstrations but the supernatural power of God to sustain us with enough for today.

How like our untrusting natures it is to want God to bless us to the point where we no longer need to depend on Him. Obscurity provides no such favor, but it does show us God's faithfulness. We must learn by experience that He is trustworthy and dependable. His sustaining hand carries us, and we learn to rely on and love Him for it. Here, our gifting cannot sustain what God is building in us.

Obscurity allows us to see not just our weaknesses but also our strengths in a sober light. Obscurity also provides a sober view of God. What a profound gift this test is. Consider it pure joy then whenever you face these kinds of trials.

> **In obscurity He indwells and encourages us with intimate tenderness. His miracles in this season tend to be daily provision.**

Tips to help us do well on this test

Obscurity is one of heaven's greatest treasures if you can recognize it. It will be the death of selfish ambition, so work with Holy Spirit as He leads you.

Don't despise the smallness of the service or the humility of your surroundings. Great treasures lie hidden in darkness, for the Kingdom is like the smallest of seeds which, when planted, can become the greatest of trees. Practice doing things that only God can see.

Kingdom impact often proceeds from obscure service. If you discover that no one but God noticed the excellence of your service to a broken few, rejoice, for His eye on you is all you need.

> **Kingdom impact often proceeds from obscure service.**

Psalm 75:6 This I know: the favor that brings promotion and power doesn't come from anywhere on earth, for no one exalts a person but God, the true judge of all. He alone determines where favor rests. He anoints one for greatness and brings another down to his knees. (TPT)

Chapter 8

The Test of Praise

PARABLE

After the King's whispered encouragement, Jethro was a different horse. He carried himself with confidence. Not quite the swagger of the naïve but a more assured, inner confidence. Over the next few days, he was assigned all the prominent jobs. He was asked to be a show horse for the visitors to the King's stables. He had to stand in a regal pose, dressed in the finery of the King's cloak after having been groomed for a solid two hours that morning.

Young people admired him, and most of them let out an astonished gasp the first time they saw him. "What a fine animal!" their parents would say and Jethro could see that even though one of the grooms was explaining the role of the King's horses, the people's eyes seldom left him. Sometimes he found himself wishing that the trainer would just be quiet and let the people talk to him and admire his shiny coat.

In the afternoons, he was excused from the rougher and more menial tasks assigned to other horses because they wanted him to look good the next day. Vincent came in one night looking particularly tired and his coat was full of mud. Jethro allowed himself a little smile and perhaps even a condescending air as they passed one another.

"What a good day that was," he said looking out of the sides of his eyes without really turning his head to acknowledge his friend.

"I'm glad you had a good day," said Vincent. "Mine was awful!"

"They are sending me back to be on show tomorrow, probably all week," said Jethro.

Vincent's lack of enthusiasm left Jethro feeling a little let down.

"He should be happier for me," thought Jethro with a self-indulgent toss of his head.

The week went on like this with the crowds casting admiring looks at Jethro. "That must be one of the great horses," said a young boy to his father.

"No, son," his father replied, "He is still a trainee, see he has no golden disk on his forehead that marks graduation and service to the King."

"Oh," said the little boy clearly losing interest in Jethro.

Jethro was angered by this. In his mind, he was already a great horse and although it was true that he had not saved the King's life or rendered any other service to the crown, it was inevitable that he would. "Why can't they look past a little thing like a golden disk and see me standing right in front of them?" he thought.

Over the past few days, he had become intoxicated with the praises of his visitors. He had secretly begun to relish each affirmation. He repeated these to himself, quickly forgetting the less flattering remarks. He wondered how he could repeat these to the other horses in the stable without appearing to be boastful. He found that with each new visitor, he expected adulation for just standing there. When they did not exclaim about how regal or powerful or beautiful he was, he found that he harbored animosity toward them.

In a quiet lull between groups as the trainer led him away to the water trough, he had a thought. "After two hours of grooming and this beautifully tailored cloak of the King's, any horse would solicit admiration. Just being here and taking up this position causes admiration."

The thought unnerved him. "No, I'm not like all the rest," he finally told himself, "I have something that the others do not and the crowd's praise is uniquely justified."

As the week drew to a close, Jethro hoped that they would assign him to be on show again and was secretly amazed and a little hurt that they did not. When they announced that the following week another horse was to be on show, Jethro easily came up with six areas in which he clearly outshone that horse.

"Why don't they see my superiority?" he fumed. "The crowd clearly sees what these trainers seem incapable of seeing. No other horse has received the praise I receive, and it's not as though it isn't helping the Kingdom. When I do well, it reflects well on the King."

It happened slowly in his heart. It wasn't as though in one day Jethro turned bitter and began to measure every slight or praise towards himself. It was that by the end of that week Jethro was frustrated, angry, and measuring himself against every other horse. He especially began to measure himself against those who wore the golden disk.

"I think I'll do far more than that one did," Jethro said to himself, "And that one over there couldn't come close to my strength or speed."

The trainers and other horses did not know that this pressure was building up inside Jethro or that he was likely to blow up over small slights.

The other trainees found Jethro's attitude difficult to deal with. When they approached him openly and with a sense of friendship, he was guarded.

Jethro's growing need to be esteemed was eating him up inside. His soul began to be burdened in the middle of his assignment, and he became sullen and spiteful.

Things really came to a head the last day of the assignment when a large crowd stood around Jethro, listening to his trainers talk and gazing in wonder at the way Jethro looked and posed. Jethro basked in the glow of their affection and praise. His poses took on the posture best suited to bring out his strengths and purposely meant to hide any weaknesses. If anyone in the crowd pointed out a specific attribute, Jethro turned to show off that attribute best. As he was engaged in showing off for a little girl who admired his mane, a trumpet call grabbed the crowd's attention.

"The King is here!" the announcement flashed through the crowd. Within a few short moments, the crowd had run to the other side of the large parade ground to get a glimpse of the King's return from the fields. Jethro was affronted.

"It's just the King returning," he thought to himself. "He's not even dressed in his fine robes." Jethro caught himself in the middle of this thought. He was shocked that it had entered his mind. "If I care more about how I'm viewed than the King, then something is wrong with me." He knew that he would have to make some changes.

His week ended with great praise for his outward performance, but in his heart, Jethro felt shame and anger at himself. "I'll never accept praise again," he thought. Somehow, treating himself harshly gave him relief from the guilt he felt. "It's simple," he said, "When I get praise, the King does not."

Uncle Malarok saw him trudge dejectedly into his stall and came over to speak with him.

"Why the long face?" he asked.

Jethro told him of his week, and Uncle Malarok smiled a knowing smile. "I understand how you feel. When you receive praise, it's a test to be sure, but not receiving any praise at all is not the answer either," he said. "You will have to learn to receive praise when you deserve it and to give praise when others deserve it. Nobody is in the spotlight all the time and no one but the King deserves to be."

"Why does the King use horses like us who are so susceptible to pride? Why does He even bother with me?" Jethro asked.

"Because He loves us. There is not a horse in the world who is not susceptible to these things, so the King trains us to conquer them in his service."

To himself, Jethro said, "I'm not sure I'll make it through the training to find out if it's worth it."

PARABLE DISCUSSED

The test of praise is one of the most vital tests we must face and conquer. This test shows us our hearts and it exposes our need to be different, special, better than others.

> Proverbs 27:21 The crucible for silver and the furnace for gold, but man is tested by the praise he receives.

Each time we are praised in Jesus's service, we are writing a pop quiz on our hearts.

"David has slain his tens of thousands" was as much a test for David as it was for Saul. Saul had to deal with jealousy, but David had to deal with arrogance and the slow slide in his heart towards entitlement. Perhaps this is why he had to endure his season of obscurity. Perhaps this is why the Lord added to him those who were the outcasts of society. If we do not guard our hearts in the middle of praise, we may need the anti-venom of obscurity to find the plan of God again.

> **If we do not guard our hearts in the middle of praise, we may need the anti-venom of obscurity to find the plan of God again.**

The call of God for David to be king, so clearly and emphatically stated in front of his family, became easily entangled with the flush of success and the open doors of favor and praise. These can turn an eager desire to pursue the call of God into a headlong pursuit of personal glory. It is precisely because we start out in purity that this blind spot can so easily entangle us.

The people in your life will inadvertently set up these pop quizzes by their comments and praises of your life and ministry. Their praises may be genuine and well-founded. They are not wrong in and of themselves. In fact, the Scriptures require honor for honorable things and respect for the respectable. The Bible requires daily encouragement of one another. The problem is not the praises, the problem is how our hearts digest them. God scrutinizes the flutter of each heart tested through the praise of well-meaning saints. Next time you're praised, be aware of the test in that moment.

> **The problem is not the praises, the problem is how our hearts digest them.**

The key is not to refuse all praise as a matter of course. The assumption that this will bring more glory to the Lord is erroneous. God is not glorified in the absence of our accolades; He is glorified when we demonstrate wisdom and bear much fruit. We need to learn how to respond maturely to praise. We need to extract from it the nutrients necessary to encourage and motivate us onward but to pass on those parts that draw our hearts to arrogance.

A mature and gracious response that accurately honors God is a learned skill. When you use your gifts in service to others, it's natural to receive a compliment. To say, "That was all the Lord, and I had nothing to do with it," is to create a strange and false impression to the person meaning to honor you. Acknowledge the praise with a genuine word of thanks. Highlight others who were involved in your task and be authentic as you praise the nature of God. Inwardly, offer your honor to the Lord and ask that He guard your heart in humility.

If we are not guarded, the praise of men seeps into our hearts, and we sip from an intoxicating cup. David was a young general in Saul's army, sitting at the king's table, married to the king's daughter, hobnobbing with Israel's military commanders, and cheered by thousands. The hero giant-killer must have found it difficult to consider others better than himself (Philippians 2:3). I'm sure David never set out to be arrogant. He was merely doing what he felt he should. It was his devotion and faith in God that had achieved his notoriety. But even his purity of heart did not exempt him from this test.

Well-deserved and well-meaning praise has an alcohol content far higher than any drink on earth. Sip it slowly. It is very difficult to sip regularly from the chalice of praise and not to feel its intoxicating effects on our hearts and minds. Be alert.

> **Well-deserved and well-meaning praise has an alcohol content far higher than any drink on earth. Sip it slowly.**

If we ingest praise without check, we will not maintain the sober view of ourselves that the Scriptures require. (Romans 12:3) This is the first danger of the applause of the crowd. We believe what the press agents and marketing departments are saying about us. This creates an arrogant spirit in us, eager to compare ourselves with others, enamored with our trophies. We condescend in our minds to others we think are inferior, and criticism becomes our natural fruit. Our hearts are drawn to praise and esteem, and when these are not immediately forthcoming, we smart at the insult. This arrogance blinds us. We cannot see the strengths of others because they are hidden behind the glow of our own glory. This false glory also hides our weaknesses from our own eyes, even when they're apparent to everyone else.

Drunk people laugh at their own jokes because they see things very differently from the sober. When they do hurtful things, they often are unaware until the next day. Paul warns the Corinthians about this in his rebuke:

> 1 Corinthians 4:6 Now, brothers, I have applied these things to myself and Apollos for your benefit, so that you may learn from us the meaning of the saying, "Do not go beyond what is written." Then you will not take pride in one man over against another. 7 For who makes you different from anyone else? What do you have that you did not receive? And if you did receive it, why do you boast as though you did not?

Our success before God is determined by how well we achieve His will, His honor, and His fame.

People who live in this intoxicated state are like those who think they are rich but who do not realize their poverty and nakedness before God. What a powerful deception this is. God is so faithful to convict us of it and spare us a path of destruction. In the end, our success before God is determined by how well we achieved His will, His honor, and His fame.

Tips to help us do well on this test

Praise is tricky. While we all need affirmation and acknowledgment for the good things we do, praise can skew our perspective. To retrieve the nutrients from praise without letting it pull you off course, try this: whenever someone praises you for something you have done or some part of who you are, graciously thank them for their kind words and immediately offer that praise to the Lord in your heart. Say, "Lord, this praise belongs to you. Help me to receive it and think about it rightly. Align my heart with your will. Amen." External graciousness and internal submission to Jesus are the antidote to praise pride. Take the remark to the Lord, and you will often hear Him agreeing with the praise you received. Offering your praise to Him sanctifies it for you.

SECTION 3

Working with Jesus

(The Lesson of Team)

Colossians 1:16 For in him all things were created: things in heaven and on earth, visible and invisible, whether thrones or powers or rulers or authorities; all things have been created through him and for him. 17 He is before all things, and in him all things hold together. 18 And he is the head of the body, the church; he is the beginning and the firstborn from among the dead, so that in everything he might have the supremacy.

Learning the lesson of teamwork starts with learning to keep in step with Jesus, by embracing what He is doing, how He is doing it, and the people He chooses to do it with. Let's explore some more tests for working in team.

Chapter 9

The Test of Perspective

PARABLE

The next week, the trainers ran around with a strange apparatus. They had all the horses congregate and put them into teams and a harness that held two horses. Jethro was teamed up with a smaller horse whose stride was short and who was quite a bit slower. His name was Yegor. Each team was required to run through the course set up for them. Jethro looked Yegor up and down, frustrated that he was teamed with a horse of such obvious weakness. Yegor was short, and so the harness between them pulled mercilessly on Jethro's high back. If Jethro wanted to proceed without irritation, he found that he had to slow down and prefer Yegor. This lack of pace wore at him more than the harness had.

"Let's go!" shouted Jethro as they started their course. He meant to win the fastest time even if he had to drag Yegor through the course. Jethro even tried to lift up the other horse entirely and only succeeded in getting their harness entangled, which required a trainer to come and help them out. Yegor looked at him with strangely knowing eyes which only caused Jethro to fume and snort his frustration while they waited for the harness to be reset. Once they got going again, Jethro found that when he took the outside line, which enabled him to go faster, and Yegor went on the slower inside track, all was well. At these times, Jethro was encouraging and happy, since he had finally found a compromise that still allowed him to shine.

When they turned toward the other direction and Yegor had the outside track, Jethro hated it, frequently tripping and bumping into Yegor because he kept trying to force him to do more. At these times, he was an absolute nightmare to be around. He snapped and snorted his derision with the course in general, and at Yegor in particular.

"This is impossible!" shouted Jethro, "I cannot be expected to bring my best when harnessed to you!"

By the end of the course, Jethro had slipped and cursed and huffed his way through. They did not do very well, and in fact, were among the slowest teams.

That night Jethro called Uncle Malarok over and begged him to partner with him in harness the next day. "I've already passed this test," laughed Uncle Malarok, "It's your time to learn, besides Yegor just asked me for another partner tomorrow as well. You two will have to get it together or you both lose."

"He wants to get rid of me?" Jethro was incensed.

The next day, while they were harnessed together, Jethro whispered under his breath, "I hope you have got it together after you messed us around so badly."

Yegor whinnied loudly and turned on Jethro with fiery eyes and curled lip. "Me? You better get it together with all your pomp and heirs and arrogance. You kept slipping and doing only what made you look good. You are an inflated windbag who could not work in a team if your mane depended on it!"

Jethro stood stunned. That wasn't true. Was it?

Yegor continued, "Yesterday, I warned you five times of what was coming, and you ignored me every time. Each time you slipped or went the wrong way, and we looked like idiots. I looked like I was not working with you, but it was you who destroyed our chances. All you care about are your chances."

Soon, they were on the starting line again and Jethro looked nervously at Yegor out of the corner of his eye. He saw a small horse for the first time and realized what it must have taken for Yegor to have made it thus far without all the natural advantages of height, speed, and strength. Jethro realized Yegor had to have relied on cunning and skill and superior eyesight.

"Maybe he can make a contribution," thought Jethro. They started the course, and it went much better. Jethro paced himself to Yegor and found that the footing was much surer at this speed. They never missed one turn and never slipped once. To his surprise, Jethro found a different delight in the success of the team. He started to rely on Yegor's strengths, and was in turn surprised when Yegor called out for him to go faster. They finished at a mud-flying pace to the applause of the instructors.

"That's the best time today," shouted the timekeeper, "Now, that's a team."

"Thanks for your help," said Yegor in between panting breaths.

"No, thank you for your help. I wouldn't have seen that limb around the last corner if you hadn't warned me. You saved us."

The next morning brought a complexity as more harnesses were added to the team and four horses were teamed together. Jethro eyed the other two horses that he and Yegor were tied to with skepticism.

"We won yesterday," said the fourth horse, a big Grey. "And we came second the day before that. We'll show you how it's done."

"Lean on my strength and listen to Yegor here," said Jethro, "And we'll help you, too. "

"No, you listen to us and we'll show you how to pace yourselves," said Garth, the third horse.

And so it was that around the newly formed team, a disgruntled and combative air cast a shadow on their individual strengths. Soon, they were off on a new course none had ever seen. They jostled and bumped and slipped their way through. Twice, they strained against one other, each horse set in a different direction with none ready to give way to the others. The first time, Jethro managed by sheer strength to pull them with him and they reluctantly decided to run with him. The second time, however, they joined together to counter him, each refusing to surrender to the other. The result is that they stood still, looking awkward, straining but going nowhere. It was the laughter of the trainers and the other horses that jolted them out of their standstill.

Jethro asserted himself again, and they ran on until they encountered a blocked passage and had to retrace their steps. Eventually, they emerged and finished, beaten, exhausted, and humiliated. They turned on each other with harsh words. They discovered there was more than enough blame to share. Each one could not wait to be released from the harness.

As they were released, Garth reared back and kicked at Jethro and then at the other horses. One of the grooms ran in too close and caught a flying hoof in the ribcage. When Garth was brought under control, he stood huffing and glaring at the rest of them.

"I will never get into a harness with you again," he declared, and by the look in his eyes, Jethro knew he meant it.

The chief trainer approached Garth and stroked his neck gently. "Come on," he said to the horse, taking his reigns. To every horse's surprise, the trainer led Garth out to the large paddock at the edge of the King's fields. When the trainer returned, he looked sadly at the rest of the trainees, "If you are to stay in the training, you must learn to ride in team. But it is your choice."

That night, Uncle Malarok came by with his most irritating smile. "How are things going?"

"They are impossible! No horse could work well with them. Why are the trainers punishing me by putting me in with the worst team of grumblers and back-biters they can find?"

Uncle Malarok's laugh woke some of the sleeping horses up. "You sound just like me when I first had to learn the lesson of team. I hated it at first but now I rely on my team for their strength and wisdom and camaraderie more than ever."

"But you are one of the greatest horses, perhaps even the strongest alive! How can you rely on them? They are weak," said Jethro.

"Their strengths are different from mine, not less. No one is strong in everything and none of us has everything the King needs. Take Yegor for example, his eyesight is the best around, but he is not too strong. If strength is the thing we always needed, then he does not stand much chance of being useful in the Kingdom.

"But sometimes seeing far is the most important thing to help the King. Yegor will shine then, and you will need him. When strength and speed are imperative, you will have your chance to shine. Don't assume that your particular strengths are the only ones useful to the King, Jethro. You must value what the King values. It is, after all, His Kingdom. Your perspective needs to change.

"Will you serve the King only if it allows you to look good and shine? What happens when the King's best interests are served, and you don't look good, but He does? Are you still willing to serve when it has no upside for you?"

Jethro had no answer.

PARABLE DISCUSSED

God will test our perspectives to ensure they match His. Wrong perspectives about our own or other people's worth are damaging to the Kingdom. Relying on our own strengths seems to be one of the easiest things to do. Conversely, we fear that recognizing other people's strengths will hold certain problems for us. If we acknowledge their strengths, will it place us in a weakened position or diminish our influence? We can get concerned that others are infatuated with their strengths and oblivious to their glaring weaknesses.

This typically leads to a culture where we are sparing with praise but loud with faults. No one flourishes in that environment, and we all tend to be defensive and combative when corrected. The Scripture holds a celebrated view of others and calls us to do the same. We are to consider others better than ourselves.

> **Philippians 2:3 Do nothing out of selfish ambition or vain conceit, but in humility consider others better than yourselves.**

If we cultivate a glorious picture of ourselves, we pursue our own ambitions at the expense of the team God has placed us in. It becomes easy to chafe at the "restraints" other team members impose upon us.

Fortunately, we are a unique part of a whole. Our strengths can make a significant contribution and our weaknesses ensure that we stay reliant on the Lord and other members of His body. My strengths and weaknesses all have redemptive purpose.

> **I am a unique part of a whole. My strengths and weaknesses all have redemptive purpose.**

It is easy to narrow our perspective to assume that ours are the only important strengths and therefore devalue our team members. The gospel does not a call us to uniformity but rather to revel in the glorious God-given abilities of our teammates. Excel in your calling but turn down the dazzling light of your own perspective to include other people's strengths. Include, also, the weaknesses in you that Holy Spirit chooses to reveal.

Do not mistake a call to teamwork as an excuse for a personal lack of excellence. Be diligent in the pursuit of your unique calling, excel in your specific strengths, and understand that for all your uniqueness, you were still designed to work in team.

Certainly, there are many things I could do on my own with much more speed and freedom. The moment I add another person to my life, the moment I am in harness, I make myself ready to experience gospel living. It is here that the love of God demonstrates itself in its greatest brilliance. When I have to be patient and forgiving with others, rejoice in their success, show humility and selflessness, demonstrate gracious and gentle speech, the love of God is made manifest in my life, and I start to live in love and in God. Being in community is indispensable and our perspective in the middle of it is vital.

We are the people who have been promised that one will put a thousand to flight but two can put ten thousand to flight. An exponential synergy occurs when we unify in team. Our strengths combined amount to significant productivity. Our strengths submitted in a Spirit-led team have eternal possibilities that far exceed our personal best. Not only are our strengths maximized in team, but if we have the correct perspective, we honor and encourage one another's strengths. In this culture of love and honor, we find the greatest personal expression.

> **Our strengths submitted to a Spirit-led team have eternal possibilities, far exceeding our personal best.**

Moreover, we are protected in team by shared strengths and perspectives. We are forewarned by others, their strengths become ours by association and we learn to trust and use their strengths. We find that their competence in the areas of their strength rubs off on us. Team members, who were formerly weak in specific areas, learn by being with people highly skilled in those same areas. Getting up once we've fallen is much easier with a teammate's help. In the often-lonely landscapes of the calling of God, there is nothing like the fellowship of a true friend. Jesus sent His disciples out in two's, and even Paul the apostle shied away from open doors because he was alone (2 Corinthians 2:12). God takes this team idea seriously.

> **In the often-lonely landscapes of the calling of God, there is nothing like the fellowship of a true friend.**

So how can we change our perspective to align with God's? It is a deliberate choice to see others as He sees them. He sees someone for whom Christ died. Their value has been established by the price God paid for them. He redeemed us with the precious blood of Jesus Christ. He bought us out from under sin and the law to be free people whom He calls the glorious sons of light. We are His beloved, the ones on whom He chose to lavish His love. We are warned repeatedly not to devalue those for whom He died, thereby destroying His work in their hearts. (Romans 14:15; 1 Corinthians 8:11).

All of the gifts God graces our lives with are intended for service. Teams are imperative for this to be possible. Our strengths, gifts, and abilities find their greatest expression in a body and are celebrated best within that culture of honor. We gain a correct perspective when we can recognize the strengths and gifts of others and celebrate their place in the team. When God sees them, He sees the gifts He gave them as He formed them in their mother's wombs. If our perspective is to match His, we must train ourselves to see what He gifted them with and find a way to include their strengths in our journey. Practice recognizing other people's strengths out loud in their presence. Say good and honoring things about people behind their backs and let the grapevine work positively to encourage them.

This requires me to get out of my own sphere of influence, my own perspective and frame of reference, and to see another's. Ask questions of your friends about what they believe God has called them to. Investigate their longings and passions.

God most often works in us the deep convictions that align with what He wants us to do (Phil 2:13). Not everyone responds well to the call of God because the call of God grows progressively more costly. The intrinsic value of having God as our great reward obligates us to let all else diminish. Those who have given themselves over to die in order that they might live discover the great joy of working with other people in the same decision. Dying to my own glory, I awake to His. Dying to my own applause, I am included in the glory reserved for the King and those who serve Him well. Dying to personal acclaim, I am rewarded with greater success in a team.

> **God's call on our lives grows progressively more costly.**

Tips to help us do well on this test

Developing eyes that can see what God has gifted others with is a massive gain in the Kingdom. Jesus only said what He heard His Father saying and He only did what He saw His Father doing. What is God doing in the people around you? As Jesus was sent by His Father, so He sends us. We should be doing what we see Him doing. Look with prayer at the people around you, and ask the Lord to give you His eyes to see what He is doing in their lives. Soon you will see hope and bright futures in everyone you look at. When you see how God has gifted people, you start to expect it and call it out of them. This is powerful for them and for you. It is the basic building block for teamwork. Seeing other people in the spirit is imperative.

> 2 Corinthians 5:16 So from now on we regard no one from a worldly point of view. Though we once regarded Christ in this way, we do so no longer.

Chapter 10

The Test of the Harness

PARABLE

After Garth was replaced by a new horse, their team training continued. The harness knitted the four horses together like a single unit. They learned to trust one another and to lean on one another's strengths. They were even moved into stalls adjoining one another and often ate together.

One day, the King came out to view them, and Jethro and his teammates were excited to prove themselves. It had been rumored that the team who did the best together would take the King out in one of His carriages.

The course was a newly designed one which the trainers had created to test the teams to their fullest. None of the teams had ever been through it, and the air was tense with excitement. By now, Jethro had learned not to speak in condescending tones to his teammates as though he was the strongest. Now, rather, they looked to each other and encouraged one another's strengths.

"We are going to need your eyes today, Yegor," said Jethro.

"I'm going to have to rely on the strength of your legs," came the reply.

"What do you think, Sebastian, is there a plan?" asked Attlan, the third team member.

Sebastian, who had replaced Garth, had proven himself well able to keep up, but he was very quiet. He was a thinker and a planner, which at first had frustrated Jethro because he seemed uncertain. But the team had come to appreciate him over the last few days when, after watching a few other teams, he made suggestions and comments that proved helpful in getting their team through some of the most difficult obstacles. It had been hard for Jethro to listen, because his first reaction to most difficulties was to employ his great strength and bust a way through. Many times, this resulted in them being stuck or injured. Sebastian had made suggestions that had made tough obstacles look laughably easy. Jethro's team was coming in first most of the time.

"Let's hang back a bit and let some other teams go first," suggested Sebastian.

While this didn't sit well with Jethro, the rest of the team were in agreement, so he went along. Sebastian and the others watched as team after team made a start and engaged the obstacles they could see from the start line. Part of the course disappeared beyond their line of sight and it was here where most teams seemed to take a long time.

"If we start out running as fast as we can, we can beat that first obstacle's boom before it comes down and then, Attlan, we need you to lean hard right and help push us around to be aligned for that second one," suggested Sebastian. "Jethro will drive us up the hill to the third through that mud and we'll stay to the right side of the puddle since it's shallower there. I suggest we slow down before going over that rise because all the teams fly over that hill, and we don't know what's on the other side." He gave all of these suggestions not with an heir of command but in a spirit of cooperation. Everyone received them and each was ready to go.

"Yegor, when Jethro is carrying us up that hill, we need you to look ahead and tell us what you see," continued Sebastian, "All of us will be trying to smell what is over that rise."

One of the trainers finally came over to check their harness and led them to the start line. They all looked over to see the King smiling and watching from the side.

"Go!" shouted the trainer, and they were off. They shot from the start line without hesitation. They each knew what they were to do, and they raced past the first obstacle before the boom was even a third of the way down. Attlan leaned hard right and ran almost in a line at odds with the rest of the team, but it produced a tight right turn that most of the other teams had not been able to manage. With the second obstacle comfortably cleared, they lined up for the third atop a long slope. Jethro dug his hooves in and gave a solid driving pulse for the rest of them.

As they were about to enter the third obstacle, they all smelt blood ahead, and Yegor shouted, "I caught a glimpse of what's over the hill and the road splits left and right. I saw blood to the right."

"When we get to the top, we slow down and go left!" shouted Sebastian.

With the third obstacle done, they slowed at the top of the hill and as they cantered over the top, they saw a large, frightening figure that had been made to scare teams away from the left pathway with low overhanging branches. All of the other teams had turned right here and for some who had come over the hill at full speed, it had meant they could not turn in time and had grazed their sides and legs, leaving blood smears.

Without anyone saying anything, the team turned left, and Jethro called out to Attlan behind him, "Lower your head when I call out." They approached the low hanging branches with speed, "Now!" shouted Jethro and they both lowered their heads. As they were going at a reasonable pace, they only had to stay lowered for two steps and they were through.

As they ran on, they discovered a great burst of exhilaration as each of them made their contribution, and they ended the course amidst the cheers and applause of everyone standing around. They had finished way ahead of every other team and the King applauded the most. The "well done's" and "way to go's" resounded as they bowed their heads and breathed hard to regain their breath.

The King walked over and said, "Tomorrow this team and I go out riding in the country." With that, the day's exercises were suspended for them and they were taken back to the stables to be fed and groomed.

As he was being brushed down, Jethro noticed that there were places where the harness had bitten into his skin and chafed him. The groom brushed him down and applied ointments to soothe these places. In more than a few places, Jethro noticed that his coat now showed signs of having been in harness. In fact, he was in harness so often these days that the marks never receded.

"I am marked by the King's harness," Jethro thought. He found the thought a good one, even though it marred his personal appearance. He found a distinct comfort in the fact that he was in service of the King.

They awoke to a bright day and a growing excitement in their bellies. After they fed, the grooms came to take each of them outside. A groom led Jethro to the side of the field where the paddock started. As he stood and stretched, the groom began to brush him down.

"What a sorry sight," came the derisive shout from the other side of the paddock fence. Jethro looked up to see a group of paddock dwellers looking on and discussing him loudly.

"He used to be a good-looking horse," said one, "But now look at those ugly marks all down his sides. Why do they do it?"

"We are also loved by the King. We eat the finest of grain and have this great paddock to run around in, but they are all scratched up and marked by those harnesses."

"Hey Jethro," shouted one of the horses, "Why don't you just get out of that program and come over here? I get to eat what I want when I want and basically, I rule my own life. There is plenty of water and fruit for the taking. Why brutalize yourself for the sake of a small disk on your forehead?"

Jethro looked at them and had to admit that each of them now looked a good bit better than he. They had no scratches or marks on their bodies. They looked healthy and strong and were happy all the time. He did not have much space on his body where he did not bear the marks of his training. The harness and traces had left cruel looking scars all over his flanks. It was also true that he only ate when they gave him food and only what they gave him. The constant running and hard training had left not an ounce of fat on him, and he had a certain look about him that the paddock dwellers did not have. Jethro thought about the joy of being able to decide for himself what he wanted to do and where he wanted to go and for a second, his heart imagined life in the paddock.

Just then, a hand rubbed him along his neck and on his muzzle. Thinking it was the groom, he didn't pay it too much attention until he noticed the looks on the faces of the paddock dwellers. They stood slack-jawed and silenced as the King continued to scratch Jethro's neck. The King leaned in and whispered to Jethro, "You have been doing very well Jethro. You and I are going to have many adventures, battles, and victories. I like your heart." Jethro was thrilled to hear his name on the King's lips. The King continued, "I have much more for you to accomplish. I have great plans for you, but you must stay the course. Let's go."

With that, Jethro was led away in the sight of the paddock dwellers to be placed into the silver and gold harness reserved for those horses honored by the King. Jethro didn't say anything because nothing needed to be said. His flanks may not be unmarked, but it was him and not them who was pulling the carriage of the King. His muzzle still felt the touch of the King and his heart still burned within him at the King's words.

PARABLE DISCUSSED

The test of the harness is one of the last freedoms we want to give up. If I am fully yoked to the cross, it means I will be constrained to do things and go places I would prefer not to. It also means a significant loss of personal freedoms. I discover the truth of the phrase "I am not my own, I have been bought with a price." It also means that the team I am connected to in the Kingdom will be seen before I am, and the applause will go to us all. This is a surprisingly tough choice for most of us. Do I surrender to the benefits of the team and thereby lose some of my individual recognition, or do I press for personal fame at the expense of the team? The truth is that in team, you will be recognized most accurately. For it is only in team that our strengths show up against other people's needs. When we try to accomplish this without accepting our role in team, we just end up comparing ourselves against others. In team, our service is received with grace and gratitude. Outside of team, we recognize people for their failure at this test.

It is a Kingdom principle that those who serve well will bear the marks of that service. We are promised victorious procession, not protection from every scratch. As part of our service, we embrace a loss of freedoms. "Where others may I may not," becomes the realization of everyone pursuing God's call. Paul recognized the marks of the call on himself and others. He bore in his body the consequences of his particular call. Those who ushered in the presence of the King in the early church all were aware that they were servants and bond slaves of Jesus Christ. Each of those today who will usher in the King's presence will eventually know the harness of His call and the imposition that it makes on our personal lives.

> **"Where others may, I may not" becomes the realization of everyone pursuing God's call.**

In His great offer to mankind, the call God offers us all, there are many who receive the call to salvation. Those who accept the call to salvation experience great joys and benefits and let go of those things that are detrimental. The power of the gospel to dispel darkness makes its impact on everyone who has experienced salvation. Life changes and all things become new. Our perspectives change and we are alive to God for the first time in our lives. What a new birth this is! Of course, it is not without its challenges, and we are expected to exercise our will in agreement with the deep work of grace that has happened inside of us. We cooperate with what God is doing in us by changing some outward behaviors to match the inner revolution that has occurred.

Next, we understand the call to sanctification. Of the many who accepted salvation, a fewer number accept the deeper call to outer sanctification. Those who do, experience a greater level of the inheritance of peace and grace that is theirs. Under the guidance of the Holy Spirit, they learn a different way of thinking, speaking and living, and revel in the cleanliness of hearts and hands. This move into sanctification is a process of agreement with the truth that we were already made holy by Jesus. It includes the renewal of our minds and the casting off of what belonged to our old selves. It will extend until we see Jesus face to face. It requires our cooperation and agreement.

> **Not everyone who hears God's call to salvation, responds as well to His call to sanctification.**

We choose to follow God's promptings, which means shunning some things that others may do freely. Where others may be under no constraint from the Lord, He may require a much stricter standard from me. This is often due to the particular wiring of my personality and the inroads the kingdom of darkness had made in my life before. Jesus said that we can loose and bind things in our own lives and in His Kingdom. This is not just by saying something is bound or loosed but also by direct surrender and cooperation with the leading of Holy Spirit.

Those who are diligent to tremble at God's word make themselves useful to the Master. The Scriptures say they will be used for noble purposes. (2 Timothy 2:20-2). If a man cleanses himself from ignoble things, he is ready for noble works. While we work on our own lives, we discover that the people God has put in our lives will be a great help in areas where we do not shine. Their strengths are a guard when we feel weak.

In many ways, this call of sanctification is a call to a group. It's a team sport. For Scripture teaches that a little leaven can work through the entire dough. So, we encourage one another and spur one another on to love and good deeds (Hebrews 10:24). We pray for, rebuke, bear the burdens, encourage, love, and help others in our harness to present everyone pure in Christ.

> **Not everyone who hears God's call to sanctification, responds as well to His call to service.**

Next, we tend to hear the call to service. Of those who received the call to sanctification, there are fewer who press deeper into the calling of God to service. This is where we start to use our gifts and strengths to serve others. Here we begin to lead. Jesus equated leadership with servanthood. These are the people learning the faithful administration of the grace of God on their lives. God wants all to experience the joys and depths of this call. Those who answer it serve others for their good, and delight to see the fruit of that service.

When people consistently accept your service, you have become a leader in His Kingdom. Jesus promised us that our call would not be different to His. John 13 shows us a picture of what we might expect in Kingdom service:

> John 13:3 Jesus knew that the Father had put all things under his power, and that he had come from God and was returning to God; 4 so he got up from the meal, took off his outer clothing, and wrapped a towel around his waist. 5 After that, he poured water into a basin and began to wash his disciples' feet, drying them with the towel that was wrapped around him. . . 12 When he had finished washing their feet, he put on his clothes and returned to his place. "Do you understand what I have done for you?" he asked them. 13 "You call me 'Teacher' and 'Lord,' and rightly so, for that is what I am. 14 Now that I, your Lord and Teacher, have washed your feet, you also should wash one another's feet. 15 I have set you an example that you should do as I have done for you. 16 I tell you the truth, no servant is greater than his master, nor is a messenger greater than the one who sent him. 17 Now that you know these things, you will be blessed if you do them.

Jesus, in the moment of revelation that His Father had placed all things under His power, the revelation that creation awaited His command, took a towel and a menial servant's position and exhorted His disciples to do the same. He said that we could not be greater than He but that we can aspire to be like Him.

Service is part of the call of God and not just the service on center stage in front of the spotlights and the applauding crowds. It is also the service to washing dirty feet in secret borrowed rooms. I don't know anyone who has accepted this call who is not marked by it. There is a humility to them. They are able to bring their considerable strength and use it in service to people of lesser capacity. Responding to God's call to service requires our cooperation and an ongoing decision to surrender to that role. This is the service offered to God for the sake of His people, trusting that our reward will be with our God.

> **Not everyone who hears God's call to service, responds as well to His call to sacrifice.**

Those who have accepted service are then offered sacrifice. Those who accept this call discover the freedom and beauty of following Jesus in realms of faith and power they had not known. They learn the joy of sharing the ministry of Jesus and come to sacrifice gladly to see the Kingdom grow. The act of sacrifice cements the truth that He is worthy. Jesus becomes ever more valuable to us because of this calling. Even a cursory reading of the gospels shows this call of Jesus to make sacrifices for Him and His Kingdom.

The Kingdom fires are fueled by the sacrifices of personal gain, reputation, comfort, family, fortune, and future. If you accept this call, others may look at you with a mix of pity and scorn, seeing the scars of your journey.

To some who have learned these lessons, God offers the call to suffering. These souls experience the fellowship of sharing in Jesus's sufferings. The calling to suffer is the last nail on the coffin of our flesh.

As 1 Peter 4:1 says " Therefore, since Christ suffered in his body, arm yourselves also with the same attitude, because he who has suffered in his body is done with sin."

Not everyone who hears God's call to sacrifice, responds as well to His call to suffering.

It makes Jesus's victory complete in us and His Kingdom paramount. The Scriptures do not view this calling with gloom, but measure it rather as an honor.

Philippians 1:29 For it has been granted to you on behalf of Christ not only to believe on him, but also to suffer for him, 30 since you are going through the same struggle you saw I had, and now hear that I still have."

Some people will misunderstand this call as faithlessness or the inability to stand on the promises of God, but I believe that the suffering outlined here is a co-laboring function. Our lives will bear the scars and marks of the call when others may run free. We will bear the presence of our King into arenas where people have not experienced Him.

Simon Peter was crucified head down at his own request. Andrew, the brother of Peter, was severely scourged & tied by ropes on an x-shaped cross where he hung two days before he died. James, the elder brother of John, was beheaded with a sword. John, the brother of James, was the only one to die of natural causes, but not until he'd been thrown in boiling oil and exiled to the isle of Patmos. Philip of Bethsaida, Jude (Thaddaeus), Simon the Zealot, and Bartholomew were all crucified. Thomas (Didymus) was lanced by idolatrous priests and burned up in an oven. Matthew (Levi) was axed to death with a broad axe. James (son of Alphaeus) was thrown down from the Temple tower but did not die so he was then clubbed to death with a fuller's club at age 94. Matthias (the 11 remaining Apostles chose him by lot to replace Judas) was stoned and beheaded. For all eternity, they will bear the marks of their devotion to the Lord.

All along this deepening calling of God, we have the right to decide our own participation. We sign up willingly, if not eagerly, by saying yes to more of the call of God. Along with each yes, we discard an element of personal direction and we gain greater measures of eternal freedom. Where others may, I may not, for I am constrained by a different set of values. Other Christians may walk in areas of choice that are barred from me because of my choice. This is what Jesus told Peter on the beach as He restored him. The deeper you go into the call of God, the less freedom you will have, and when you are old, they will lead you where you don't want to go. Inevitably, the deeper into the call of God we go and the closer to Jesus we get, the more we pour out our lives in service to others. Jesus demonstrated this with his life of service. He said a servant is not above his master.

We will share the cup of Jesus, which is to lay down our lives in order that others may be brought into freedom. We share that call along with all the glorious benefits of intimacy with Him, and we will be the people who usher into the King's presence to our homes, our workplaces, our neighborhoods, our cities, and beyond.

Each one of us must answer the question for ourselves whether it is worth it. Without a vital walk with Jesus, we may consider it too large a price to pay. The secret is to press into intimacy with Him. In this place lie all the treasures that make the price of our calling seem like light and momentary afflictions.

> **Along with each "Yes" to His call, we discard an element of personal freedom.**

Standing alongside these sons of the Kingdom are paddock dwellers. They do not bear the marks of the call, not because they were not called, but because they did not choose to respond at that time. Some of these may follow your example and some may not.

We have different gifts according to God's grace, and they will stand or fall before their own master one day. We must not judge others who make a different choice—that is between them and God. But we cannot let their decisions affect ours. Each of us must choose to embrace the limp that Jacob had, wrestling with God over these issues.

Those who know what it feels like to share intimacy with Jesus bear their scars as badges of honor.

Tips to help us do well on this test

This is not a chapter about personal sacrifice and dying to self so much as it is a call to become enamored with Jesus. Only in the context of a rich relationship with Him do any of these sacrifices have value. We are not called to sacrifice ourselves as a fulfillment of some legal requirement. We are called to know and love Jesus. Just as earthly parenting requires sacrifice, so does a love for your Father. Out of that real relationship, giving, serving and sacrificing are natural expressions.

Don't think that you can forgo the relationship and expect your sacrificial acts to be impressive. Seek the Lord out, spend time with Him, cry out to Him, withdraw often to be with Him, and out of the overflow of your relationship, it will be your joy to work with Him. You will discover He is still the same person He showed Himself to be when He walked the earth as a man, loving the hurting, caring for the poor, comforting those who need it most. If we want to walk with Him, we will join Him where He is and embark on the adventure of our lives at His side.

Matthew 11:28 Come to me, all you who are weary and burdened, and I will give you rest. 29 Take my yoke upon you and learn from me, for I am gentle and humble in heart, and you will find rest for your souls. 30 For my yoke is easy and my burden is light.

Chapter 11

The Test of Value

PARABLE

"We have come to that time in the training for you to decide whether you want to stay or not," said Uncle Malorok.

Jethro looked around at all the horses who had come this far and marveled at the difference in them since they had first arrived. On that day they had been eager, full of life and looking their best. Now they looked calmer, a little scratched up, but filled up with a newfound confidence. All of them bore marks of the harness and the reigns.

"It does not get easier from here on out," said Uncle Malorok. "In fact, now the real tests begin. Today you have the day off to roam around the King's estate and decide whether you want to continue."

Jethro and his team found one another and discussed where they should go. "Why don't we go over to the edge of the stream over there?" said Sebastian. "If we lean over the fence, we can still reach some of the ripe apples growing in the orchard."

On the way, they passed nearby the paddock and saw some of the trainees in discussion with some paddock dwellers.

"Let's put a stop to that," shouted Jethro angrily, but as he turned to confront the group, a voice of great command stopped him and his friends.

"Jethro!" Uncle Malorok trotted over to him. "You leave them be," he said, "They have the right to make this decision for their own lives."

"But if we convince them, we can save them from the lies of the paddock dwellers," Jethro charged back, being as forceful as he could without showing disrespect. He knew Uncle Malorok would not look kindly on disrespect.

"You may indeed convince them temporarily, and as long as they are in your presence, they will abide by your conviction. If they never face it for themselves, they will never truly be free. There will be many, many opportunities in the future for their hearts to be turned from loyalty to the King. The lures of comfort or fame or prosperity are powerful motivators that can cloud even a great horse's heart. They must win this battle here.

This day off is more of a test than any you have yet faced. It gives them opportunity to discover the secrets of their hearts and to make their own decisions about the direction of their lives."

"But if they choose to leave now, they will have suffered for nothing and they will not bear the King's carriage," said Yegor.

"That is true, but they will have a sense of the King's heart. If they are going to turn back, it's best they do it now before they are recognized as established horses of the King. If they are recognized and then turn back, they bring much more disrepute and shame than if they freely decide now. The King is not a brutal owner. He invites us in to share His adventures, but He does not force us to them. We either come volitionally in agreement or we will cry foul whenever we have to endure hard times or tough assignments."

"What kind of test is this?" said Jethro. "Give me a physical challenge anytime, tell me what I must do, however hard it may be, but don't give me all this psychobabble."

"It's not psychobabble," laughed Uncle Malorok, "It is the fundamental decision we must make for ourselves. Do you want to be a servant of the King?"

"Yes!" said Jethro, Sebastian, Yegor, and Attlan almost in unison.

"Do not answer so quickly. Surely your training thus far has shown you both the rewards and the price tag of pulling the King's carriage?"

"I still want to be a King's horse," said Jethro, "And not because I am naïve. I have seen and felt the weight of that price tag and I have decided that I will take the whole package, the glory and the pain. I am the King's horse." Jethro stomped his hoof and lifted his head in unison with this emphatic statement.

"You may have just passed," smiled Malorok and walked away.

The team ran over to the orchard and spent the next few hours relaxing and eating the sweetest apples they had ever tasted.

Some of the horses wandered around near the paddock and spoke with the paddock dwellers about how good life was in the paddock. Some of the horses avoided the paddock dwellers or even picked fights with them, defending their choice to stay in the program. Several times, Uncle Malorok walked up to groups of horses to give them advice and to allow each horse to make his own decision.

Jethro's mind began to wander, and his heart yearned to be with the King again. They had shared such great moments when they had taken the King's carriage out. They had stopped by a stream and the King had un-harnessed the horses and spent time with each one, riding each one and talking with them. These were the best moments of Jethro's life. It felt like the King knew him exactly. When he was with the King, his heart felt at peace and yet exhilarated all at the same time. He longed for that moment again.

"I wonder what the King is doing right now?" asked Jethro.

"Why don't we go and see," suggested Attlan.

The four horses trotted off toward the palace to see if they could discover the whereabouts of the King. Each of them had been impacted by their time with him, and Jethro could see that each one of them wanted to spend more time with him, just as he did.

They searched in all the usual places a horse could go but they did not see him anywhere. When they asked one of the chosen ones if he had seen the King, he suggested they try over at the mud pit.

"There's no way the King would be at the mud pit," snorted Sebastian. "He's the King!"

But they ambled over in that direction. To their amazement they found the King surrounded by two stable boys, knee deep in mud and dung from the horse's stables. He was laughing and had stripped his shirt off. The King looked up at them and smiled. The four stood too amazed to say anything or even to move.

"Just in time," said the King. "One of the noble's sons lost some important jewels down here and we've been digging through this pile to find it. But I don't want to leave this pile out here like this, so I need a team to help me drag it off to the fertilizer pile over there." The King pointed to a large pile across the field.

The four rushed to get into the traces and soon found themselves in the pit, mud and dung splattered, pulling hard against the harness. Gradually, they began to move the huge pile of mud and dung that had been set on top of the large tarpaulin attached to their harness.

"Thanks team, you have done me a great service, and I will not forget it," shouted the King as they passed him. Smiling, he held up two large sapphires that had been lost.

"It's amazing what treasures are hidden in dark places," he whispered in Jethro's ear and then he was gone, walking back to the palace to get cleaned up.

The team dragged their burden clear across the field. On the way, they heard the derisive cheers from the paddock. "Look at that great strength and teamwork," they mocked, "Let's call them the dung squad."

Horses all around the field looked up, undecided whether to laugh or frown. Many laughed from both sides of the paddock fence, but some looked on them with awe. Then the four noticed a strange thing happening. All of the chosen ones stood tall facing them with one hoof bent low in the sign of respect. They held their heads up high and strained all the more eagerly to the traces.

"We are about our King's business," puffed Jethro, "And we will do it with pride."

When they were finished, grooms came to fetch them and they were led away to be washed and brushed. That night, they were each given a bowl of sugar cubes with their supper.

"Compliments of the King," said one of the groomsmen.

The talk at supper time among all the horse was all about indecision and stress. Should they stay on or go? Was it worth it for what was ahead?

The only four horses who did not share this concern where Jethro, Sebastian, Yegor and Attlan. They stood happily confident together, sure of the King's pleasure and convinced that a few slight inconveniences were worth the time with the King. Where others had spent their day in idleness and chatter, they had spent most of their afternoon in the mud and dung with the King.

Uncle Malorok came over to Jethro after supper. "Do you know why you four were honored today by the chosen ones?" he asked.

"Tell me," said Jethro.

"We honor what the King honors and we value those who align themselves with Him. His bidding is not always glamorous, but it is always important. You provided a vital service to all of us even though it was not pleasant."

Jethro was humbled by his good fortune. "We didn't mean to provide that service. We just wanted to be with the King and he was in the mud and we just did what he wished," Jethro tried to explain.

"Your desire to be with the King will continue to keep you that fortunate in the future as well," said Uncle Malorok.

Jethro thought back to some of the paddock dwellers who had looked on them with respect when they returned from the mud. Some even had sugar cubes in their mouths, much like the ones Jethro and his team had been given. "Uncle Malarok?" Jethro asked. "Are there good horses in the paddock?"

"Oh yes," smiled Uncle Malorok. "There are many good horses there. Some even return from the paddock to be of great service to the King. And some are of great service within the paddock. The secret is to watch what the King honors and honor it, too."

"So, we did well today?" asked Jethro.

Uncle Malorok said very seriously; "Well done, young Jethro."

PARABLE DISCUSSED

A beautiful transformation happens inside sons and daughters who choose to bear the King's presence into this world. The transformation of their minds shows up in the way they learn to view and value things with Kingdom eyes. It is impossible to serve Kingdom goals with an earthly mindset. Part of the riches of our glorious inheritance is that we are invited to share the mind of Christ. He wants our thoughts to be His thoughts and our ways to be His ways. Jesus started by calling Himself the light of the world and then, when He was about to leave and institute the church, He called us the light of the world. We are to carry on His ministry.

Jesus taught us that the value we place on the Kingdom of God will obligate us to exchange all the riches of our house in order to possess it. In the parables of the pearl of great price and the treasure hidden in a field, we understand that we pay for what we value. This implies that if we value the wrong things, we will spend our time and resources on non-essentials.

> **We spend money on what we value. Let's make sure we value the right things.**

We need to press into the presence of God, and in cooperation with Holy Spirit, allow a shift in our minds. We need to be renewed into heaven's values. We need to deliberately press away from the pattern of this world, as Romans 12:2 teaches, in order to understand the will of God. We become trustworthy servants to the extent that the things that God values ring in our hearts. The world of God's Kingdom is at odds with the Kingdom of this world. We must make a choice, because straddling the fence is not an option. Jesus said:

> Luke 16:13 No servant can serve two masters. Either he will hate the one and love the other, or he will be devoted to the one and despise the other. You cannot serve both God and Money." 14 The Pharisees, who loved money, heard all this and were sneering at Jesus. 15 He said to them, "You are the ones who justify yourselves in the eyes of men, but God knows your hearts. What is highly valued among men is detestable in God's sight.

The things men value most are often detestable to God and at odds with His purpose. The deceitfulness of religion will coax me to an outward form of obedience but allow me to harbor wicked values in my heart. Therefore, it is imperative that each of us face this reality and confront this giant of our values. Holy Spirit is faithful to add grace and power to our hearts for this great transformation, but He seeks that we co-labor with Him.

> **The things people value most are often detestable to God and at odds with His purpose.**

We are called to evaluate everything. We must learn to value what the King values. He gives us this space to decide for ourselves. This is an intensely personal and internal decision. How much do I value the King and His Kingdom? This sounds like the most obvious choice, but life and service will put the undecided to the test.

What we value is an anchor for our souls. It is the blueprint for us when the service is heavy, and the task is unpleasant. At these times, there are often those who stand close by, seemingly in the same environment, without any of the pain you experience, who offer advice. They often downplay the importance of your task and show disdain for the sacrifices you make to ensure your values. They tempt you to give up on your perseverance, toil, and current discomfort for the promise of ease.

Pain has an amazing ability to limit our focus. Marked, personal, internal choices help keep our focus stretched beyond the boundaries of pain and discomfort. They remind me why I am doing what I am doing and help me press past the ridicule of others. Personal times with the Lord are the key to helping us make these decisions. An understanding of Jesus's pleasure motivates us toward more service.

> **Internal choices help us focus beyond the boundaries of pain and remind us why we do what we do.**

This is why the Scripture in the New Testament shows Jesus more interested in our hearts than our actions. While both are vital, it is what we do in secret that the Kingdom rewards. A close read of Matthew chapter 6 shows this. Our secret giving, prayer, and fasting bear the Father's smile. A constant stream of forsaking instant gratification for eternal rewards starts to add up, and our hearts and our minds turn heavenward. If I expect my reward to come from heaven, my heart is drawn to my treasure.

Our constant sojourns to the secret place begin to bear great public fruit because His presence abides with us and we bear that presence everywhere. What you choose and value internally will become apparent to all around you.

> **Our constant sojourns to the secret place bear great public fruit.**

We are called to encourage one another against sin's deceit and to consider how we can spur one another on towards love and good deeds. Ultimately, each of us will adapt to the environment we live in. If that is a white-hot "love Jesus with your whole heart," culture, we find it easy to love Him. Yet it is what we do with our free time that makes the biggest difference. It is what we value in the secret places of our hearts that will determine our ultimate usefulness in the Kingdom. The dividing line between those who know it's worth it and those who don't is intimacy. Those who have met with the King in secret rejoice in His service in public. Sometimes that public service seems menial and unimportant. It is at these times when our values are tested the most. But no matter the task, when we're walking in our calling, we gain a sense of security and assurance in our faith.

1 Timothy 3:13 Those who have served well gain an excellent standing and great assurance in their faith in Christ Jesus.

Tips to help us do well on this test

Offer your heart and mind often to Holy Spirit. Invite Him to fashion you and guide you into a clearer manifestation of Jesus's nature in you. Those who have their hearts set on what the Spirit desires are freed from worldly desires.

Our hearts and minds can be totally transformed when we give Holy Spirit lordship in our lives. He gives us the mind of Christ. How precious and valuable people become, and how easily love flows between us when He is Lord. Offer yourself again and again as a living sacrifice to Him and He will make the road clear as you walk in all your calling.

> **How precious and valuable people become, and how easily love flows between us, when Jesus is Lord.**

Galatians 5:16 So I say, walk by the Spirit, and you will not gratify the desires of the flesh.

Chapter 12

Going Beyond Obedience

PARABLE

"We're near the end of your training," declared the head trainer to the horses that stood in the field. "We have more trainees at this point than ever!"

Jethro looked around at the group. Less than a third of them remained. His heart sank at the thought of the horses who had left. Good horses, strong horses, horses he had admired in many ways. He looked out towards the King's paddock where they were now installed, trying to see if he could recognize any of them. Jethro no longer viewed them with arrogant disdain. Those were friends of his, horses of distinction. He knew that many of them had incredible skills and he wondered whether they felt the loss of opportunity to pull the carriage of the King. Again, the shadow of sadness threatened to take his mood.

"I hope we can stay friends," he said, to no one in particular.

While he was still looking at the paddock, he saw a familiar figure. The King came walking past the southern edge of the paddock, waving to the horses. He came into the middle of the field where the trainees were standing in harness. While still a long way off, he sat down in the middle of the field with his back towards the group.

"Let them rest for a while," shouted the head trainer and the horses were slipped from their traces and given the freedom to roam about.

"Be ready when we call you back!" called the trainers.

Jethro glanced back at the King. "Could I just walk up to him?" He thought, "Would He want me there? Would I bother him if I approached?"

Before he could think too much about it, Jethro walked out to the King in the field.

"What do you think you're doing?" called one of the trainees.

But Jethro pressed on, his heart beating fast. "I want to be with the King!" was all he could think. As he grew closer, he struggled with himself. "What should I do? How should I act?"

When he got close enough, the King turned his face toward him with a great smile.

"I hoped you'd come," was all he said and rose to embrace Jethro. "You and I have so many adventures ahead of us," said the King. "I love the heart in you, but I especially love that you came to seek me out."

Jethro was stunned. This was a test as well.

He saw out of the corner of his eye that the rest of the trainees were watching them from a distance, and he noted how most of them stood back, not daring to come closer. Only Vincent came forward carefully, almost pretending like he didn't notice them, so that if he were reprimanded, he could be off quickly. But when he was near, the King laughed at him and held out his hand. Vincent looked every bit as amazed as Jethro at the warm reception.

"This is the part I love the most," the King said. "It's not the ruling, the court, or the dignitaries, but this connection with you. Come,

let's go for a ride." The King swung himself up on Jethro's back. He leaned low over Jethro's neck and said, "let's go, my friend."

Jethro ran out of the field onto the country lane that led into the woods.

When they finally stopped by a stream, they were both exhilarated by their run. Jethro neighed in excitement and his voice was joined by the laughter of the King.

"I will always be here for you," promised the King and Jethro knew he meant it.

Finally, they walked back into the field where the rest of the trainees and trainers waited in groups around the edge. Jethro noticed a subtle shift in their manner towards him. He had been accepted and honored by the King and they honored him in agreement.

"Come find me again when you can," whispered the King into Jethro's ear, and with a smile, he walked through the line horses and into a carriage that had drawn up in their absence.

"What did he say to you while you were gone?" asked one of the horses.

"Oh, nothing much," said Jethro. He wasn't trying to be secretive but couldn't decide what to share. It had all seemed so personal, and sharing it seemed to reduce it somehow, like he was bragging. The meeting left him humbled, as though every bit of competition and arrogance had been removed by the King's kindness.

A whole new world opened up in Jethro's mind. "I can please the King not just by obeying orders or instructions, but by my connection to Him. Sometimes, he is moved by what I want."

This idea captivated Jethro. All of the training seemed like a tiny price to pay for the privileged relationship that now lay open to him.

Jethro realized he would have to manage the other horses and the trainer's expectations while he pursued time with the King. Over time, when he was alone with the King, their understanding of one another grew and a magnificent synergy was formed. They connected and they shared things he had not shared with anyone before.

Yet when they were together with other horses and trainers, the King would spend time with others, performing His royal duties. Sometimes, all it took was a look from across the room for Jethro to understand the kind intentions of the King toward him. But in these public settings, even when their mutual connection was on full display, Jethro discovered that the King made every effort to include others and invited Jethro to do the same.

Yet at every opportunity, when his duties were completed and he had freedom to roam, Jethro always walked out to the field or the wood looking for the King. When the King was there, they would have fun together. The King often talked with Jethro, explaining what was going on in the Kingdom or voicing a concern. Mostly, they just spent time together.

On his carriage rides, the King often asked for Jethro personally or included him in the team to pull his carriage.

Occasionally, Jethro would be subjected to ridicule or scorn from a paddock dweller who was sleek, happy, and carefree. At these times, he would often feel the hand of the King gently patting his neck and he would laugh out loud and say to himself. "It's worth it, it's definitely worth it."

PARABLE DISCUSSED

People don't last in their callings because of the perks. People make it because they meet Jesus on the way. Even the most exciting areas of your faith journey will have its own tedium. Even the most basic boundaries will have their share of pain. What keeps us going is not the same motivations that a presence-free career could offer. No, Kingdom life draws its joy from the King Himself. Time with Him impacts our productivity and motivation.

Right before He went to the cross, Jesus changed the relationship He had with His disciples.

> John 15:15 I no longer call you servants, because a servant does not know his master's business. Instead, I have called you friends, for everything that I learned from my Father I have made known to you.

Learning obedience is something even Jesus had to do, but our calling goes beyond mere obedience. He is interested in relationship, understanding, and connection. This moves Him as much as our obedient service. It was not enough to be servants. He wants sons and daughters. Mere dutiful excellence falls well below His desires. He is looking for a bride to captivate Him.

Those who choose to bear the Presence of the King must learn to love His Presence in secret places. Those who bear it most have spent the most time in it.

Those who bear the Presence of the King have learned to love His Presence.

The realization that He longs jealously for you will change the way you view Him and the way you act around Him. God can easily overwhelm anyone He created. He makes a scene just by showing up. This is how He will deal with the enemy. He will merely show up in glory (2 Thessalonians 2:8). He limits those moments, He woos us toward Himself, He offers, and He waits. Those who know Him and who take the time to seek Him out discover the great joy of His open arms. Glorious connection and fellowship arc available to anyone who come to Him, to anyone who asks.

In John 13, Jesus gives us a story that speaks of the intimacy available to us even in the middle of troubled times. Jesus is speaking with His disciples at the last supper. He is aware that Judas is going to betray Him and of the sufferings that will result that evening. He tells them about the betrayal, and because John has positioned himself at Jesus's side, he is uniquely able to whisper a question and to hear the answer. No one else heard it because they were not close or bold enough to ask.

> **John 13:21 After he had said this, Jesus was troubled in spirit and testified, "Very truly I tell you, one of you is going to betray me."22 His disciples stared at one another, at a loss to know which of them he meant. 23 One of them, the disciple whom Jesus loved, was reclining next to him. 24 Simon Peter motioned to this disciple and said, "Ask him which one he means." 25 Leaning back against Jesus, he asked him, "Lord, who is it?" 26 Jesus answered, "It is the one to whom I will give this piece of bread when I have dipped it in the dish." Then, dipping the piece of bread, he gave it to Judas, the son of Simon Iscariot.**

Why was John privy to this information when all the others were not? It's because of the way he positioned himself. John was bold enough to ask the question. He called himself the disciple whom Jesus loved. He leaned on the relationship he had with Jesus.

Peter was still appointed to lead them after Jesus left the team. The issue of closeness to God does not imply that you will be the highest place in every assignment. The calls of God are His to determine and divide. But we will have the opportunity to seek Him out, not only for power and wisdom, but also for intimacy.

Jesus often withdrew Himself to lonely places to pray. Ever wonder what those prayer times were like? A son longing for His Father, embracing their unity, reveling in His touch, listening to His advice and instruction.

> **Jesus was a son longing for His Father, embracing their unity, reveling in His touch, Listening to His advice and instruction.**

We are called to do the same. And these times bring Him so much joy. The test that virtually no one recognizes is this one. The calling of the King to join Him alone, not especially to receive orders, not for a targeted benefit, but just to be with Him, to love Him and to get to know Him.

John 17:3 Now this is eternal life: that they know you, the only true God, and Jesus Christ, whom you have sent.

The gifts we have been graced with are the work and plan of God. They have been given in the measure that pleases Him. They can be developed by diligence and humility, for He adds grace to the humble. How much we know Him is the fruit of our own choice. Seeking Him is our privilege, made available to all without prejudice but only seized by a few. His call still goes out, "Whosoever wants to, come!" but it is often cast aside by the pressures of life and the busy-ness of our agendas.

The King still waits in the center of the field for those who dare to join Him. His response to those who do is always the same. Full of laughter, acceptance, and adventure.

Tips to help us do well on this test

Recognize the moments when the King calls you out to be with Him. Not every offer will be overt, some will be covert. He loves the secret meetings fueled by desire. He responds to those who go out to lonely places in search of Him. He always enfolds the hungry hearts.

If you have heard nothing else from this book please hear this, the whole story of God and man began and continues in this deep truth of eternal romance. It fuels the plan of salvation, it underpins God's dealings with you, it frames our expectations of Him. We were destined to love and be loved by Him. Give full reign to your love of Jesus, don't hold back, and don't surrender your authentic desire for Him to any religion or legalistic yoke. Stop trying to perform for God. Be a lover of God. The only kind of performance Jesus loves is the kind that flows from intimacy.

Ultimately, you will choose what He is worth to you. Many are content to settle for an obedient life of religious observance. Some will usher His presence into their world to see true transformation. Which will you choose?

Chapter 13

Gold Disks on Faithful Heads

PARABLE

The day came when the trainers and King's horses gathered in a circle and all the remaining trainees were brought together. "This is the day you graduate," said the trainer. "You have made it through, you have passed the tests, you are ready to be recognized as the King's horses."

A great and yet calm elation surged through Jethro and all the others.

None of his former ambition remained, none of his old arrogance had made it through the training. There were no more I dreams of glory and honor for himself, the only ambition that remained and burned deep within him was to do well by the King. "I want Him to be proud of me," was all he could think.

"You will be presented to the King tomorrow in the grand ceremony and will receive the disks of gold, the mark of your acceptance and calling. Family, friends and many others will also join the ceremony, for the King has declared it an important day."

After they were dismissed Jethro sought out Uncle Malarok. "How long have you been a King's horse?" he asked

"Oh, many years now," said Malarok. "It's almost time for me to retire."

"You? Retire?" snorted Jethro. "I don't believe I'll ever see that."

Malarok smiled and nuzzled Jethro. "What a fine horse you have proven to be. You will live up to everything that has been provided for you. But I am making ready to depart this important role. I just want to make sure that after all these years, I continue to bring honor to my King, even if I am in retirement."

A great swell of pride overtook Jethro as he watched his uncle amble off. With new eyes, he saw the gentle limp that betrayed his age, and the sway in his tread that spoke of his weariness. Suddenly, he didn't look like the invincible Malarok, he looked like a dignified King's horse, faithful and kind, gentle and true. "That's how I want to finish my race," thought Jethro.

The next day, Jethro was bathed and groomed so that his coat shone, and his mane was brushed so that it flowed. The best blanket bearing the King's crest was put over his shoulders and he was led out with the rest of the trainees and the King's horses to partake in the grand ceremony of the King.

They marched in synchronized lines into the stadium to the murmur of the crowd. Although Jethro felt the crowd, like a living being, shouting and murmuring and jostling, his eyes sought out only one person. The King, standing center-stage on a podium said, "Today, we are here to accept into my service, seven more horses who have passed the training of these past months. "They will henceforth be known as King's horses and shall have the privilege to bear the presence of the King."

The crowd erupted in shouts and applause, but Jethro's eyes filled with tears so he could not see them. "It's amazing," he thought, "I don't care for their praise at all."

One by one, the seven were called to stand before the King. He reached over their heads to fit the gold disk on each. When it came to

Jethro's turn, the King whispered in his ear, so softly that no one else could hear. "I am so proud of you, Jethro. You are greatly loved by Me. We have many adventures ahead of us. Well done!"

When they got back to the stables, they were set in harness and asked to pull the King's carriage to an important state dinner. No special parades, no particular delicacies at their meal, no one clapping for them as they left with the King. All that was left was a lifetime of dutiful service with one great reward: the King's friendship.

As he rode, Jethro kept hearing his uncle's question in his mind. He laughed and responded out loud. "So worth it." Then he leaned into the next turn.

PARABLE DISCUSSED

When Jesus entrusts us with position in His Kingdom, it's often different than we imagined when we first started out. The times we are in the spotlight, doing what everyone admires, are given meaning by the many moments behind the scenes, the faithful walk-in quiet places, where mostly only He sees. We didn't merely decide for ourselves the authority He bestows, we grow into it through the processes of God. To be entrusted is a big deal in the Kingdom.

1 Thessalonians 2:4 On the contrary, we speak as those approved by God to be entrusted with the gospel.

1 Timothy 1:11 that conforms to the gospel concerning the glory of the blessed God, which he entrusted to me. [12] I thank Christ Jesus our Lord, who has given me strength, that he considered me trustworthy, appointing me to his service.

Those who know they have been entrusted with a specific call by God will seek to be faithful in it, just as Paul exhorts in Corinthians.

The mature and seasoned veterans speak kind words as they straighten their backs and run the last of their race with dignity. The young ministers who have passed training look forward to a life of faithful ministry. In these moments of intersection, when their relay is almost done and yours is just beginning, take some time to honor the veterans and learn all you can from them. Their lives have overflowing wisdom that can save you a great deal of pain and time if you are willing to humble yourself to glean it from them. The increasing treasure that they have amassed in heaven draws ever stronger on their hearts so that they long for what is to come when they see Jesus face to face.

To be found faithful is a great day for those who have been called to it. What a privilege it is to be dedicated and set aside to serve the King. Obeying His word and trusting His voice above all others. Forsaking the praise and derision of men to seeking after His opinion. Surrendering your gifts to His purposes rather than for personal gain. If you make this choice to enter the training and pursue a life of service to Jesus, no matter what that looks like in your unique sphere, we salute you.

What you have decided is worth it, even though it may not always be celebrated. Don't let the lopsided value system of this world have any power to discourage you. Yours is a high and a heavenly call. Yours is the most honored of all roles.

When you endure and submit to God's training, you get to usher in the presence of the King. You get to speak to and for the King. You get to bear the gold crown of service to our King. Yours is an eternal reward.

> 2 Timothy 4:6 For I am already being poured out like a drink offering, and the time for my departure is near. 7 I have fought the good fight, I have finished the race, I have kept the faith. 8 Now there is in store for me the crown of righteousness, which the Lord, the righteous Judge, will award to me on that day—and not only to me, but also to all who have longed for his appearing.

The crown of righteousness awaits you, because after all is said and done, you have been spoiled for the world. Now there abides in you a deep and growing longing for His appearing.

You have a race marked out for you by the hands of your Creator, the mountain-maker, earth-former, the One who calmed the stormy seas, and the champion of all ages. All the glitter of this world cannot come close to the thrill of His voice, or of His touch, or life in His presence.

You have chosen the better path, to give yourself away on behalf of His plan. You have done really well. I cannot commend you or tell of your courage enough. For all eternity, we will celebrate your life. Well done.

Final thoughts

If you are starting out in service to Jesus, find someone ahead of you, someone whose life is marked by God in a way you desire, and honor them by asking for their advice and extending your thanks and encouragement. Honor and listen to them. Dignify their time with thoughtful questions, even the ones you don't yet understand.

If you are ending your race, go boldly into the future. Don't tear down through tiredness or hurt what you have spent years building and protecting. Look up, the King is near, and He holds the victor's crown for you. He is the gracious God who waits for you with gold at the end of your race.

Let your last steps be facing forwards and give the last of your strength to Him, because He will catch you when you cross the finish line. There is no measure of honor on earth that can encapsulate what heaven bestows on those who have been in harness with the King. All of heaven will rise to honor the people who gave their all for Jesus to be lifted high.

There is no measure of honor on earth that can encapsulate what heaven bestows on those who have been in harness with the King.

Made in the USA
Columbia, SC
30 December 2023

ab224ec4-03cc-4bdf-a4df-65403f284b4aR01